Unplugged

Unplugged

How to Disconnect from the Rat Race,
Have an Existential Crisis,
and Find Meaning and Fulfillment

Nancy Whitney-Reiter

SENTIENT PUBLICATIONS

A paperback original

Cover design by Kim Johansen
Book design by Adam Schnitzmeier

Library of Congress Cataloging-in-Publication Data

Whitney-Reiter, Nancy, 1970-
  Unplugged : how to disconnect from the rat race, have an existential crisis, and find meaning and fulfillment / by Nancy Whitney-Reiter.
     p. cm.
  ISBN 978-1-59181-070-4
  1. Conduct of life. 2. Generation X--Conduct of life. 3. Sabbatical leave--Psychological aspects. 4. Travel--Psychological aspects. I. Title.

BF637.C5W485 2008
158.1--dc22

                                  2007051103

Printed in the United States of America

10 9 8 7 6 5 4 3 2 1

SENTIENT PUBLICATIONS
A Limited Liability Company
1113 Spruce Street
Boulder, CO 80302
www.sentientpublications.com

FOR BABBO AND NUNZI,

WHO NOT ONLY GAVE ME THE WANDERLUST,

BUT THE COURAGE TO KNOW WHAT TO DO WITH IT.

Contents

Acknowledgments

I am very thankful for the support and encouragement of my family, and of the countless friends I made during my travels. Special thanks to Judy Rylands and Shona MacLean for a memorable time in Africa (is that a leopard growling or your stomach?); Jill Earle for her friendship (I still want that African spice!); and Violeta Epstein (blue toenails are finally in style!).

I would also like to thank Jaime del Castillo from Proyecto ASIS and Leon Lopez Corella for their life-changing philosophies; Paul Jones, Richard Walton and the entire crew at Global Vision International for running a top-notch operation of which I was proud to be part; and last but never least, Paulo Coelho for opening his heart (and someone else's castle) to this burgeoning warrior of the light.

Gina Panettieri and Connie Shaw: thanks for believing. Barbarann Kanute: thanks for being "home" when I didn't have one (and not charging me rent!). Diyana Hrzic (because you'd kill me if I didn't). And finally, thanks to my husband Greg, who suffered through countless "I have an idea!" moments in the writing of this book, and didn't object to my sharing the painful aspects of our path together. No matter how many peaks and valleys the future holds, I can face it all with you holding my hand.

Introduction

A journey of a thousand miles begins with a single step.

—*Lao Tzu*

W HEN I LEFT MY JOB AT A FORTUNE 500 COMPANY to embark upon a year long international travel sabbatical, I thought my dilemma was unique. Why was I not satisfied with a life that, by all standards, was successful? True, as a 9/11 survivor, I had more reason than most to reconsider my life and how I wanted to spend the rest of it. As it turns out, however, I was not alone. While most of my coworkers and friends were exclaiming, "I wish I could do what you're doing," plenty of others of all ages were packing their bags. I met several of them in my travels, which took me from Central America to Africa, to various cities in the U.S., and finally to northern Arizona, where I now reside.

There is no doubt that many in our modern society are in the midst of an existential crisis. The tremendous success of books such as Po Bronson's *What Should I Do with My Life?* and memoirs such as Elizabeth Gilbert's *Eat, Pray, Love,* and the resurgence of Paolo Coelho's *The Alchemist* exemplify the inner struggle faced by many working professionals today. The ideals of previous generations have gradually eroded, leaving nothing to fill the vacuum that they have created. Corporate loyalty is virtually nonexistent—gold watches have been supplanted by pink slips, as downsizing and outsourcing have become a daily fact of life. Going to college has become an expectation in its own right. Students are pressured while just beginning high school to think about their college careers, rather than being encouraged to think about who they *are* and who they want to *become*. In addition, with the advent of globalization and the Internet frontier, the choices for what to do with one's life are limitless. The result of this is an entire generation that has rushed into life without a clear purpose (Generation X), a generation that finds itself with the rug pulled out from under it (Baby Boomers), and a new generation that is starting to burn out at a faster rate than ever before (Generation Y).

Newsweek International recently ran a feature article about this trend, for which I was interviewed. Doing the interview caused me to start thinking about the fact that while there is an emerging trend of young people taking midcareer breaks, there aren't any useful books out there to help them accomplish this or find their true path.

This book is designed to explain not only *why* career breaks are necessary in our modern, technologically driven society, but *how* to take such a break, in easy to follow steps. Each chapter includes personal stories from the author, lessons from others who have successfully unplugged, and "Small Steps to Freedom" (writing and reflection exercises designed to prepare you emotionally and mentally to unplug yourself). There is also an appendix devoted to useful resources to help you with all aspects of your journey.

Consider your purchase of this book the first small step on a lifelong journey of enlightenment. May your travels be rewarded with the greatest treasure: discovering who you really are.

Chapter One

Why Am I Unhappy?

IF YOU ARE LIKE MOST MODERN PROFESSIONALS, chances are good that, from the very moment you entered high school, you were pressured to start thinking about college choices with little or no consideration to first developing yourself as a person. Or, if college was not an option, you were then under pressure to find something to do that would not require a degree so you could get out there and start earning a living. On the threshold of adulthood, you faced a momentous fork in the road.

If you chose college, you may have found yourself in one of two groups: those who had no idea why they were there or what to study, and later found themselves trapped in an unsuitable major, or those who thought they knew, only to find out that the real life application of their degree was not as fulfilling as they had hoped it would be.

Alternately, you may have chosen to skip college altogether, and then found yourself with limited choices that you have either continued to live with or have gone back to school to try to amend. Those who end up on this route actually have an advantage: their experience in the real world work-force gives them a definite idea of what they *don't* want.

Whichever fork of the path you traveled, it's possible that you are now facing a problem. Nowhere in this period of becoming an adult have you had the time to devote to exploring *yourself*: what makes you happy, what you're truly good at, what brings you the greatest satisfaction.

If, like me, you are a child of the '80s, you have been force fed a constant stream of consumer driven goals that are based on nothing more concrete than a marketer's latest scheme.

Many of us grew up with the concept that greed is good, and have set forth on an endless path toward the accumulation of wealth to finance a purely materialistic lifestyle. If we are not able to accumulate wealth, we simply accumulate debt. According to the Federal Reserve, over 40 percent of households today spend more than they earn. The average American consumer owes about $9,000 in credit card debt, with an average interest rate of 14 percent. It has been reported that 50 percent of Americans would not admit to a friend what their credit card balances are.

We've been programmed since birth to believe that our needs are greater than they actually are—the latest toy, car, or electronic gadget is a must-have—only to be told "that's so five minutes ago" soon after we acquire it. The moment something better comes along, we are no longer satisfied by what we have. We give absolutely no thought to this pattern, and become seduced each time by the next best thing. This trend is hardly new to Generations X or Y. Observers of this facet of human nature can be traced all the way back to Aristotle, who wrote that "the avarice of man is insatiable." What is alarming is that the pace of this cycle, from coveting to rejecting, is speeding up. In addition, this mentality is spreading to areas other than consumer goods; it has become evident in our personal relationships, our spiritual beliefs, and our jobs.

Relationships

Thanks to the Internet, we are now able to find, meet, and test drive new romantic partners faster than ever before, many times without leaving our current—no longer satisfying—relationships. Who in our generation hasn't been guilty of shopping for partners on the Internet after a fight with their mate? Who among us hasn't been on the receiving end of this duplicity? I would hazard that very few could answer in the negative.

I am not against Internet dating. It is, in fact, how I met my husband. It allowed two people from very disparate backgrounds to meet—which in all likelihood would not have happened otherwise—and eventually fall in love. There is probably no person in the world better suited to me, and I would not have met him without the Internet. That said, the Internet was also a constant source of problems: each time we had a fight or broke up, we both knew exactly how many other candidates there were to fill the void. At best, it is a double-edged sword.

Just as the pace of what I call the Covet/Reject Syndrome keeps speeding up, so too does the world of artificial introductions. Not long after Internet dating started to become socially acceptable, Speed Dating came along to hurry the process along even further. Now groups of men and women can meet at a specified location and determine within five minutes or less if a person has the potential to replace their current or past mate. Like Internet dating, speed dating has its success stories.

What concerns me is the underlying symptom of which it is a manifestation: rather than working through our relationship problems, we focus on replacing our mates.

One of my favorite speakers is Ellen Kreidman, author of the *Light His Fire, Light Her Fire* series. Ellen speaks frankly about this tendency of human nature: We each have ten good qualities and ten bad qualities (ten being a randomly selected number to make a point). If you replace your mate with someone new, this is going to be true of the new person as well. They are going to have qualities that attract you in the beginning, but they will also have qualities that annoy you. Many times, it's those same qualities that attracted you in the beginning that you will later find annoying. The man you saw as vivacious and the life of the party will later be seen as self-centered. The woman you saw as nurturing will eventually be seen as stifling. The man you saw as charmingly protective will soon be viewed as possessive. Yet we are quick to replace our current mate and their set of flaws with a brand new person and a brand new set, to be discovered later. After all, we are secure in the knowledge that divorce is quick and finding a new soul mate can take as little as five minutes.

Spirituality

Many in our generation try on religions like we try on new shoes. Every so often a new concept comes along that captures our attention, if only for a little while. Sometimes, it's a very old or recycled idea. When Madonna appeared on stage toting a red ribbon on her wrist, Britney Spears and Lindsay Lohan soon followed suit, proclaiming the wisdom and insights they have gained from the ancient religion of Kabbalah. Unfortunately, the majority of the people following this fad will find that it, too, leaves a void at the core of their being. This is not a result of a fault in the belief system, but rather a reflection of the fact that the quick adoption of a new religion is an ineffective band-aid for an existential crisis.

New Age and mystical books account for an ever increasing share of the market. Alternative history is one popular category. These are books about secret societies, freemasons, and alternative religions. Steve Fisher, Vice President of ThorsonsElement U.S. said in *Publishers Weekly*, "One thing I've figured out is that it's not a big leap for a lot of the self help movement to go into religion and spirituality. People are trying to find new answers as they search for something bigger than themselves."

Dan Brown's controversial bestseller *The Da Vinci Code* (recently a major motion picture with Tom Hanks) has amassed a following of its own—not just on the merits of being an incredibly well written work of fiction, but as a result of the goddess worship religion described therein. The market is now flooded with factual books on goddess worship and the duplicity of Christianity's forefathers. Who wouldn't want to believe in a religion that sees ritual human sex as the highest form of worship? This is especially true of those using sex as an escape or to mask their pain through forced intimacy. Our generation has developed a far more cavalier attitude towards sex. Just fifty years ago, our cultural mindset was totally different. Today, many in our generation give no thought to experimenting with bisexuality and other alternative lifestyles, not because that's who we are, but precisely because we *don't know* who we are.

The Da Vinci Code mentions several alternative history books as references. One of these, *The Woman with the Alabaster Jar*, published ten years previously, sold ten thousand copies in a seven month period in 2004 (after being rediscovered by readers of *The Da Vinci Code*). According to Ehud Sperling, president of Inner Traditions/Bear and Company, "What makes *The Da Vinci Code* exciting isn't the character development or even the setting, it's the whole mystery and magic around a reinterpretation of the Christian mythos.

There's a real thirst and a hunger in our society today for a different story around Christianity." I believe this hunger is really the desire for an "Aha!" moment that will solve our internal problems.

Wicca is another extremely popular trend amongst seekers. Gene Brissie, Citadel Press's Editor in Chief, was quoted in the same issue of *Publishers Weekly*. "We've all heard the expression: 'I'm spiritual, but not religious.' In another era, people attracted to Wicca might have gravitated toward a more traditional religion. In the early days of the Reformation, for instance, the new Protestants would pick and choose from a variety of emerging beliefs. To a degree, Wiccans today also pick and choose. Wicca is nonhierarchical. There is no Pope of Wicca. Wiccans are free to mix and match beliefs. It's a community that shares its beliefs through books." Wicca is therefore highly appealing to a generation of people who have made jumping from religion to religion a commonplace occurrence.

The sleeper hit *What the BLEEP Do We Know!?* offers a new mindset. "There is no God," one speaker proclaims, "*you* are God." While the point of this truly excellent movie is about letting go of old fashioned precepts about spirituality and religion, and finding yourself at one with the universe, it is easy to see how statements like those can leave a person who is in search of answers with far more questions instead. It is virtually impossible to see one's interconnectedness with the universe if one has no sense of identity.

My concern is not Kabbalah or the myriad other choices, philosophies, and beliefs we are exploring. Exploring spirituality and new ideas is healthy and enlightening, and can actually be an important step toward getting to know oneself. My concern is the speed at which we proclaim to have adopted a whole new mindset, only to discard it when the hole we have inside fails to be filled by whichever trend we are currently following. This hole will never go away, unless and until we become *whole*. The only way to become whole is to know oneself.

Careers

The third way our generation is manifesting symptoms of malaise and dissatisfaction is with our jobs. Gone are the days of the gold watch for staying with one company until retirement. Today's young professional faces a world in which downsizing and outsourcing have become the norm: manufacturing jobs are not the only ones that have left our borders. Pick up the phone to call customer support for virtually any product and you are as likely to be speaking to someone in India or the Philippines as you are to someone in Michigan. Not even our pension funds are safe, as demonstrated by recent corporate scandals.

America is the hardest working nation in the world. According to the International Labour Organization, Americans now work more hours than workers in any other industrialized country. In just twenty years Americans have added an hour and a half a week, or over a week of extra work a year. Despite this, a RoperASW study published in the May 2003 issue of *Money* magazine found that 57 percent of Americans surveyed would rather have more money than more free time, versus 27 percent who would prefer the opposite.

In light of the fact that job security is virtually nonexistent, and that job satisfaction is also rare, these survey results are surprising. Why do we want more money, at the cost of the free time to spend it? We are a TGIF society that *chooses* to condense our free time into two days. Could it be because we wouldn't know what to do with ourselves if we had more time off? Walk into any major corporation on a weekend and you are likely to find young people working. They are not required to be there, they are "just catching up on a few things before Monday." These are the very same people that if polled, will tell you they are unsatisfied with their jobs.

Many times we jump from company to company, thinking that we will find happiness in a different environment, but never questioning what it is that we actually *do*. Frankly, that is just too frightening a question for most of us. We look back at that fork in the road, many years ago, and think of all of the time invested in getting to where we are. *How can I change anything now*, we might ask. It's too late. We have bills, mortgages, incredible amounts of debt from financing either our schooling or our consumption (or in many cases, both). We have relationships. We have fears. Our minds dismiss the notion of trying something radically difficult because it is just too hard.

Brian's Story

∞

Until the dot bomb hit in 2000, Brian had been working in a great series of IT jobs at various telecom companies. "I was making great money and had a good deal of job satisfaction. Then the dot com bubble burst and forced many of us to re-examine what we were doing careerwise."

Since Brian had risen to the second highest rank in the nation on the amateur golf circuit, he decided to take the plunge and see if he could transform his passion into his livelihood. "I realized that I found much more satisfaction in golf than I found in an IT job. What became very apparent was that the moments of satisfaction in my job were infrequent—typically

BRIAN'S STORY, *cont.*

when I finished a project—which was only about twice a month." On the other hand, Brian realized that even playing amateur golf, he always had a sense of direction and found some level of satisfaction, even on days that didn't go perfectly. "It was a very clear process for me—something that kept me involved mentally and physically. I definitely did not have this in my IT job despite the feeling of satisfaction with my earlier career."

Brian volunteered for a layoff in August of 2001. "I was getting ready for the US Amateur at East Lake GC and the ship was sinking at Winstar Communications. Immediately after I volunteered for the layoff, I knew I'd made the right choice."

Brian used the funds from his layoff to finance his first year in the amateur circuit. He learned some valuable lessons during this time. "First, there are people who really care about me and the dream that I'm chasing. They're willing to help me if I simply ask. Second, I've realized that we live to our means. I'm no less materially satisfied now than when I was making $80K a year in my IT job. I'm perhaps more satisfied because I've realized that certain material things aren't that important." A good example is Brian's shift in attitude towards personal transportation. "I used to covet the new cars with the new gadgets. Now I look at it as solely a method of transportation—if it runs effectively and totes my gear around, it's good enough for me."

When asked what activities he engaged in on his journey, such as journal writing or meditation, Brian replied, "I just played golf. Golf is its own journey of self discovery. The deeper you get into the process, the more you see it as a mental exercise. It's belief in yourself and the process that yields results." According to Brian, the process of improvement is as important as winning. "This is a difficult process to express, something I've come to know intuitively over the last few years. I believe it's a core principle for anyone trying to improve his life. For example, if your goal is to land that CEO position, you have to really want it. But the most effective way to get there is to focus on the process of improving yourself for that job instead of just trying to get it."

When asked if he's ever regretted his decision or had moments of doubt, Brian responds that even today, this is a periodic challenge. "I deal with percentages of failure where winning one or two tournaments per year is considered success—and you may not even be 100 percent satisfied with your performance when you do win. There are many down times when you know how comparatively easy it would be to slug through a nine to five day and take home a weekly paycheck."

That said, there is no question in Brian's mind that his life is better now than before his journey. "I understand the simplicity of life and the importance of the people in it. I've learned that the materialistic, market driven society is a trap that we're all being pushed into." Although Brian's career ultimately depends on successful marketing, he can't help but wonder if marketing will be the downfall of western civilization.

BRIAN'S STORY, *cont.*

Brian believes that the most important lesson he's learned from unplugging is the importance of having balance in life. "I play the best golf when my play, practice, and time off are balanced. When I practice, the more focused and goal driven I can become, the more satisfying my practice sessions." Brian has learned how to compact very effective practice into time slots that most recreational golfers find very surprising. "This allows me to achieve a balance between work, relationships, and personal time that is very satisfying. The better my balance, the happier I am in life." To follow Brian's burgeoning new career, visit his website (listed under Resources).

It's too hard to change careers; it's simpler just to change companies. It's too hard to make a struggling relationship work; it's easier to find a new mate. It's too hard to self examine and develop one's own spiritual beliefs; it's simpler to follow the latest fads. We are breeding a generation of contradictions: we have virtually limitless choices, but no one to tell us which ones to make.

Rob Thomas, the multitalented lead singer and songwriter for Matchbox Twenty, sings what could be dubbed the Generation X anthem in *Something to Be*, from his solo debut album:

I don't really want to be me no more
I need you to tell me what to stand for
I've been looking for something
Something I've never seen
We're all looking for something
Something to be

The answer, of course, is that it is not up to anyone else to tell us what to be. The answer involves finding this out for ourselves, which is nearly impossible to do with the frenetic pace we have set for ourselves. One of the greatest ironies of our work ethic and culture is that we work so hard to be able to afford a nice place to live, nice furniture, neat gadgets, and expensive home entertainment and exercise equipment, and then watch it collect dust as we spend more and more time at work in an effort to afford more things that we won't have the time to use or enjoy!

This is not to say that some people do not derive immense satisfaction from their jobs. But chances are, they are not the ones reading this book. This book is for those among us who have tried to lose ourselves in our work, in our relationships, or in radical new philosophies. And we've succeeded—in losing ourselves, that is. This book will show you how to take time out to do just the opposite—get to know yourself!

Small Steps to Freedom: Writing Exercise

On a scale of one to ten, with five excluded, rate your current level of satisfaction with your job, your relationships, and your spiritual awareness.

Now think back to a time when anything was possible for you. Does your current reality match up with that vision? Which of the above categories requires the most changes to meet that vision? What kind of changes would be necessary, and why haven't they taken place?

Chapter Two

The Need to Unplug

"O KAY," YOU SAY, "I'M READY. SHOW ME HOW TO find myself." I have to warn you that what I am about to propose to you will *not* be easy, fast, or convenient. That said, I can assure you that it *will* be the best investment of time and effort you will ever put into yourself or any of your endeavors.

In the film *The Matrix*, there is a point when the protagonist, Neo, is told that he can see things as they really are, or he can go back without discovering reality. Once he sees the truth, however, he won't be able to go back to his old life. Ever. The same will be true for you: once you unplug from our distraction packed, consumption driven matrix, you won't go back. The difference here is that you won't want to. Once you take the time to truly find yourself and what makes you happy, you'll never want to go back to the artificial world that most of the rest of the population is operating in. You won't need to move from relationship to relationship, or job to job, or play leapfrog with new religions. That's not saying that you will lead a boring life. Rather, you will find greater peace and satisfaction in doing the things that you *want* to do, not what you think you're *supposed* to do.

How can I possibly know this? The answer is simple: because I've done it myself. For as long as I can remember, I would seek answers from other people about what to be when I grew up. The person I looked to the most was my father, who, in an effort to be supportive, would give me what he believed to be the best answer: "I'll be proud of you no matter what you do." Great. Where did that leave me? For the most part, with a whole lot of choices and no direction.

I ended up choosing the path of least resistance. High school was a form of torture for me: there was a not a single group or clique I felt 100 percent part of. One week I'd hang out with the thespians and another with the punks. Perhaps the next week would find me with the Campus Crusade for Christ, and the next with a random bunch of misfits. I had the most eclectic group of friends imaginable, and most of them didn't like each other.

I used to attribute this lack of belonging to the fact that I'd been a military brat: born in Ethiopia and raised in Italy and Spain. I came to the U.S. for the very first time during that most emotionally tender of times—high school. I later discovered that this feeling of being an outsider and not fitting in was not only not unique to me, but it was a prevalent symptom in the majority of my generation, regardless of how well some people pretended otherwise.

Since I hadn't managed to narrow my direction in high school, I strongly resisted the thought of going to college. Instead, I got a corporate job, and then married within two years of graduating. I soon found out that for a girl without a higher degree, the choices were few. Not having the mindset or the personality to be a subordinate for life, I ultimately chose to go to college. Somehow—and I'm still not sure how!—I ended up with a master's degree in economics and a double bachelor's in economics and international studies. With my head full of lofty ideas about changing the world, I convinced my husband to move to the DC area.

Soon after settling in DC, I found myself with an impressive managerial position, a very good salary, a great house full of expensive custom furniture, and an assortment of equally impressive friends. My position entailed the occasional presentation to Congress and the fruits of my work even found their way to the *Wall Street Journal*. Why then, did I feel so empty?

Although I was married to a wonderful man, our union was far from perfect. The day I realized my marriage was over was a tough one. I'd met my husband at eighteen, married him at twenty, then one day eight years later, found myself across the dinner table from a complete stranger. We'd both been back to school since we got married, and our paths took us in different directions. We literally developed into two totally different types of people. I used to joke that if we won the lottery, we'd spend all of our time fighting about how to spend it. The sad thing was that it was true—we had virtually nothing in common. The news came as a shock to most of our friends, family, and acquaintances. Because we got along so well on the surface, most of them had seen us as the perfect couple. They had no way of knowing about the emotional, mental, and spiritual vacuum neither one of us could fill for the other.

For a short time during my separation and after my divorce, I attempted to stretch my own boundaries a little. I learned to play golf, which my husband had always hated. Well, I can't say I really *learned*, but I took lessons, and enjoyed them. I traveled. I joined clubs. I almost killed myself whitewater rafting. I went out dancing. I read a lot of metaphysical books. (Due to my divorce, I no longer perceived myself as welcome in the Christian world, so I sought the answers elsewhere.)

Unfortunately, I had no idea what to focus on, other than the job that I was supposed to be deriving so much satisfaction from. I did the classic Generation X hop from one fad, sport, philosophy, and relationship to another. Although I was happier single than I had been married, I was grossly unsettled. I missed the security and the defining role of being a wife. Now I could be whoever I wanted, but I faced the same problem at twenty-eight that I did at eight—I didn't know who or what that was.

My behavior during the next few years was less than exemplary. I vacillated from relationship to relationship and sometimes back again. When one relationship would become too difficult, I'd simply hop to the next. The Internet made this far simpler than it should have been. Sadly, most of the people I was meeting had this same set of issues. Either they'd been heavily scarred by past relationships, or they didn't know what they wanted out of life and were looking to *me* for answers. That was a scary thought. These relationships were like being on a boat with no oars, in dark choppy water, with neither party knowing how to swim.

I was in the midst of just such a relationship in September of 2001. We had the most amazing highs, followed by the lowest lows, weighted down by our respective piles of baggage. As Fate would have it, we were about to experience one of the most frightening events in history together, which would tear us apart, weigh us both down with even more baggage, and years later, put us back together again. I'm speaking of 9/11.

The week of September 11ᵗʰ found me in Manhattan, attending an economics conference —ironically enough billed "In a New York Minute." (The theme of the conference was economic shocks and how various outside factors affect our economy.) Tuesday the 11ᵗʰ was actually the last day of the conference. I'd arrived the weekend before, with my boyfriend in tow. After all, this was the Big Apple! There was a lot to see and do prior to attending the conference, which began on Sunday. We were experiencing one of our peaks at the time: enjoying the fine food and the electric vibe of the city. We were staying in the Marriott World Trade Center, which was part of the first tower to be hit.

As it happened, I was running late that morning and so was still in the hotel room with my companion when the first plane struck. The plan had been for me to be downstairs attending the early morning breakfast session, and he was supposed to be on the roof, shooting some panoramic shots of the city. At first impact, our instincts were screaming for us to get out of the hotel, and so we did, without our shoes, wallets, cell phones, or anything else. We just left down the emergency stairs and didn't look back.

I won't go into too many of the details here. I'm sure most people have a lot of knowledge about what those in our situation went through. There has certainly been enough television footage of the masses of people trapped in the smoke and dust, or of those making their way on foot across the Bayonne Bridge. You may have even seen me amongst the crowds, but you probably wouldn't have noticed that I wasn't wearing any shoes. I had no easy way to get back to DC and it was a terrifying twelve hours before we found shelter.

Throughout that time, my boyfriend and I worked like a true team. We listened to each other's instincts and helped each other survive. At one point, he even carried me across a field of broken glass, although he wasn't wearing any shoes himself.

When people hear about our 9/11 experiences, they almost always make the same comment. "I can't believe that going through that didn't bring you closer together!" At first,

I couldn't either. The fact is, going through such a terrifying experience and almost dying only magnified our doubts, insecurities, and fears. Is this the right person for me? Who am I? Why am I in this job? Why am I in this particular city? Should I have worked harder at my last relationship? What do I really want to do before I die? For someone who had managed to reach thirty without any answers, the events of 9/11 only magnified the uncertainty that was emblematic of my entire life. All of the issues simmering beneath the surface of our relationship finally erupted, with collateral damage on both sides. The climax wasn't immediate, however. It took almost two years to come to fruition.

During that time, we had decided to make a brand new start and we moved to a place neither one of us had ever been to before, San Antonio, Texas. When I think of those times, I remember the adage, "Wherever you go, there you are." Exactly! There *we* were—with all of the same issues we had in DC. The same types of jobs, the same fears, the same doubts, only in a new city with no existing infrastructure of friends or family. We made even worse choices and managed to hurt each other even more. 9/11 bound us inextricably together yet drove us apart with questions. It was a constant seesaw of emotions, loyalties, and uncertainty.

Eventually, we broke up, and managed to stay apart long enough for me to decide I needed a real change. Walking by my office one day, a colleague I barely knew said to me, "You look like a caged animal." I realized it was true—I felt imprisoned by the walls of my private office, imprisoned by the little gridlines on the Excel spreadsheets I stared at day in and day out.

The power to break free came suddenly. Since I was born in Africa, I'd had a lifelong fascination with returning there, but never a willing partner. Now I found myself newly unattached and with no reason not to go. I'd been half heartedly surfing the Internet for a new job, this time knowing that a change of venue was not the answer, but not knowing what else to do instead.

I came across a website that offered long term volunteer trips to all parts of the globe; one of them was a Wildlife Research Expedition in South Africa. For a fee, you could participate in this expedition for up to ten weeks even without any relevant experience, as long as you were fit and willing, and could afford the contribution. To my chagrin, there were no spaces until October, and this was March. In order to force myself not to back out, I found another program in Costa Rica that I could participate in over the summer, and then applied to both.

I could not believe the burden that was lifted from me as soon as I quit my job. What surprised me even more was the reaction from my family and friends. Not one of them questioned the fact that I was about to leave my successful life behind and travel the world. Rather, they pretty much all said, "Do it! It's what you need." The only doubters were the people who did not know me well, or who were so entrenched in the system that their negative comments were nothing but thinly disguised envy.

My sabbatical was at times exciting, at turns frightening, and sometimes even depressing. By the time I was ready to leave, my ex-boyfriend had been begging to get back together with me, or to at least come with me on my journey. Fortunately, I understood that this was something I needed to do alone, and for no one but myself. There were several lonely nights in the African bush when I questioned my choice, but ultimately I emerged from my experience with a very solid idea of who I was, for the first time in my life.

My travels to Costa Rica and South Africa took me completely out of my familiar surroundings. Rather than living in a posh apartment, I was sharing accommodations with at least a dozen other travelers. Instead of being plugged in to the world through my cell phone and the Internet, I found myself without either one for nearly six months, except for the occasional trip to an Internet cafe to let my family and friends know I was still alive. Rather than being bombarded by false goals and ideologies, I was forced to really open my eyes and experience the world that was truly around me.

During my travels, I met dozens of people, from all over the world, all going through my same type of existential crisis. When I had embarked on my journey, I had believed I was alone. That my experiences in high school were unusual. That being a 9/11 survivor made me unique. Instead, I found myself surrounded by people with similar experiences, similar questions. I will share some of their success stories in later chapters.

About a month after I had repatriated, my cell phone rang. I was astounded to see my ex-boyfriend's number on the display unit. "Aren't you going to tell me that this trip was the worst mistake you ever made?" he asked. "Not at all," I replied, "it was the best thing I ever did."

One of the truths I had discovered was how much I truly loved him. However, I hadn't expected him to be waiting for me once I returned. In fact, I specifically asked him not to wait, because I had to know that I was completely free to do this for myself, and for myself only—with no safety net of any kind. We did not communicate while I was gone, and since both my birthday and Christmas passed in that time with no word from him, I (painfully) believed that he had moved on. And I had let go.

The truth is that when you really love someone, time and distance don't make that love go away. But time and distance do wonders for emotional baggage, especially if you spend that time wisely. In the bush, no electricity meant there was no Internet, no TV, and very little communication with my previous world. I spent a lot of time writing in my journal, mostly about how I was feeling, what I missed from my previous life, and what I was glad to be away from. My journal entries show that my ex fit into both categories: I missed *him*, but not the unsettled relationship we had.

After a slow reintroduction, we solidified our relationship and are now married, quite happily. The problems, insecurities, jealousies, and other issues that used to plague us are long gone. We are two whole people. We give each other space, support each other's dreams, and gaze towards the same horizon. We wouldn't be a solid couple if we hadn't taken the time to become whole individuals first.

Am I suggesting that in order to find yourself you must do it alone? If you are not in a healthy, happy and fully committed relationship (see Doug and Cindy's story in Chapter 7), I absolutely am. I did encounter several couples who were taking an extended sabbatical together, but for the most part these were individuals who simply needed a break from the world. They knew who they were, and they understood the person they were with. They weren't there to find themselves.

If I had gone on this trip with my ex-boyfriend, I would have behaved entirely differently, had possibly no time to myself, and spent very little time in self reflection. Being alone can be scary, but it is the only way you will get to know yourself.

Many in our generation are addicted to bad relationships. There are very few who are strong enough to be alone. Being in a relationship, no matter how bad, distracts us from ourselves. We devote our energies to the other person, and can blame them or their behavior when we are feeling unhappy. For most of us, our life is one big distraction: we spend as much time as possible at work, and then fill up as much of the remainder as possible with a romantic partner. The goal seems to be never to be alone.

Once again, you are faced with a fork in the road. You could stop reading this book and go back to the unsatisfying life you've been leading up till now. You can put this book down and pick up the latest metaphysical or New Age best-seller, in the hope that it will hold a different, easier answer for you. Or, you could admit that your greatest need is also your greatest fear—the need to know and understand yourself.

This is a journey you must undertake by yourself, but you will not be alone. Once you disconnect from your artificial world, you will encounter many others on this same quest. You will have new experiences, learn new skills, be enlightened by different philosophies, and make new friends. You will also get to know a fascinating, unique, and worthwhile individual—your true self.

Small Steps to Freedom: Writing Exercise

What are the obstacles that would prevent you from taking six months to yourself? How about one month? A week? An hour?

Now, which of these are truly obstacles, and which are excuses? Which are temporary, and which are permanent?

If the only thing standing between you and living your vision was one of those permanent obstacles, could you find a way to eliminate it?

Chapter Three

The World Is Your Oyster

W HERE SHOULD I GO, AND FOR HOW LONG? The answers to these questions depend largely on how well you want to get to know yourself. Are you someone who, like me, has never really known yourself? Anything shorter than three months would be a gross disservice, merely another band-aid approach. The ideal time period for this deep of an inward journey is six months to one year. On the other hand, if you are someone who has merely lost touch with your true self due to outside distractions, anywhere from two solid weeks to a month may be all that it takes. The key, of course, lies in the destination.

It is extremely important to choose a destination that is completely foreign to you, although by foreign I do not necessarily mean out of the county. If you are a city slicker, perhaps some time spent on a dude ranch in Montana would be sufficient. I chose to call this book *Unplugged* because the more we stay connected to our existing matrix of consumer driven ideals, the harder it is to truly spend time in inner reflection.

Like Neo, we must unplug from this matrix to find the truth. I tend to favor international destinations, for several reasons.

Television

Television is perhaps the biggest promoter of our consumerist ideology. Thanks to network television and cable, changing locations domestically doesn't mean we won't be exposed to exactly the same drivel that we would watch back at home, interspersed with commercials that reinforce golden calf ideals. Overseas, if you do happen upon a television, you will be less inclined to watch it if it is in a foreign language. Should you decide to watch television, you will at least be exposed to a different variety of cultural ideals and beliefs. (You may still find your favorite shows, but hopefully they won't be in English.) The best thing to do is to avoid television completely, especially the news.

Cell Phones

As many of us are sometimes chagrined to discover, our cell phones work pretty much everywhere in the U.S. Unless you have a tri-band or similar phone, chances are you will not be able to use your cell phone while you are overseas. To most in my generation, suggesting that one give up his cell phone is akin to asking him to willingly give up a limb. The cell phone is a wonderful invention that makes it possible to be connected to the rest of the world at all times. To the person embarking on an inner journey, however, a cell phone is like a ball and chain. Sure, it may give you a sense of security while traveling, but it is also your connection to all of the things that you must detach from if you are to accomplish anything.

I'm not suggesting you pitch your phone or your wireless system. I'm suggesting that your choice of destination should be one that removes or limits that option for you. Believe me, on this journey there will be many moments of weakness in which you will be tempted to use your phone to reconnect to the world you left behind, no matter how much this will set you back emotionally. Case in point: when I began my journey in Costa Rica, even my tri-band phone did not work there. Since my trip occurred in the critical few months after the total detachment from my ex-boyfriend and was the start of my emotional journey, there were many moments when I longed to make that call, even though it would have set me back several months in the emotional progress and healing I'd made so far. When I did call him, from a pay phone in the city center, he fortunately didn't recognize the number and never picked up the phone. Though it didn't feel like it at the time, this was certainly a blessing in disguise. If my phone had worked, he would have recognized the number and picked up the phone, and a moment of weakness could have led to a total deviation from my path.

Not everyone embarking on a journey like this will be recovering from a broken relationship, so you may think this piece of advice does not apply to you. Do not be fooled! It is not just ex-boyfriends who are potential land mines on the road to discovery of your inner self. Think about it: virtually everyone you know—your family, your coworkers, even your best friend—sees the external version of the person you have been portraying, the outer shell. In the course of any communication you have with these people, you will be reinforcing parts of your former belief system, about yourself and about the world.

Naturally, I'm not implying that you should be incommunicado for the duration of your journey, especially if you will be gone several months. On the contrary, it is important to have a support system in place prior to your departure. You need to be able to connect with them to let them know you have arrived safely, and they should be able to contact you in a true emergency. But in those lonely moments you are sure to have, you don't want it to be too easy to reach out to what is only a distraction, no matter how well intentioned. It is precisely in those moments when you feel alone or scared that you must reach *within* yourself. Journaling is an excellent therapy for those times. I learned more about myself when rereading my journal entries than I have at any other time.

The Internet

As someone who has spent many years working from home, I have to love the Internet—it enables me to work outside of the confines of a cubicle while pursuing a job I love. I also keep in touch with friends around the world, read the news, do my banking, and shop for products. In short, I am your very typical member of Generation X. In a recent study, it was found that many Generation X-ers (and even more so those in Generation Y) actually view the Internet as an extension of their consciousness. "Let me just check my email" has become a weary mantra. We do it at work, at home, and on vacation. Being without email is perhaps one of the hardest sacrifices we are asked to make. I know that when my service provider experiences an outage, it feels like the end of the world. The sales of Blackberries and other wi-fi products have skyrocketed in the last several years. Being connected at all times through these gadgets is wholeheartedly perceived as vital for most in my generation.

Despite my love of the Internet and its many applications, disconnecting from it is perhaps the most important tactic while you are on this journey. The reasons are the same as those for not being in constant phone contact: you do not want to be distracted by well intentioned friends, old wounds, or existing beliefs. Like phone communication, I don't mean for you to eliminate it completely, but you definitely don't want to be in a position to access it daily or even weekly. If you are going away for only a month, then you actually *do* want to eliminate it totally. There are very few places in this country that you cannot find an Internet café. This is also true of most major tourist destinations abroad. Therefore, your choice of location has to be one that will solve this problem of easy access to temptation for you.

Travel Options

If you have read this far (congratulations!), you are probably a bit frightened at the notion of wandering off to a distant place by yourself, with no cell phone or access to the Internet. For many in my generation, this does not only seem frightening, but unpleasant to boot. It may be hard to believe, but this is precisely the mode of travel employed by those on the path to enlightenment for centuries! Jesus didn't bring any such devices with him in the garden of Gethsemane, and yogis don't bring their cell phones to the mountain top, even though there'd undoubtedly be good reception. Even so, I realize you may be saying, "But I didn't live centuries ago, I'm alive *now*, and the Internet and cell phones are my reality."

My proposed solution is to make your trip part of an organized group. If anything should go awry, you will have the support of the sponsoring organization as well as of your fellow travelers. Even though I had previously traveled to several dozen countries on my own prior to my sabbatical, I chose a group experience for my extended trips. This made sense for several reasons, the primary one being that I would be a single female traveling alone. The second reason was that I would be traveling to two countries I was unfamiliar with, and I wanted the structure provided by an organized experience. Finally, both of the programs that I was involved with (teaching children in Costa Rica and working with wildlife in South Africa) were not programs that were available to the general public. They both enabled me to sample an alternative career, without the investment and commitment usually required to be in a position to do so.

Volunteering

When most people think of going off to see the world through an organization, they most often think of groups like the Peace Corps. While the Peace Corps is certainly a worthwhile organization that offers a life changing experience, it is not for everyone. The main barriers are its twenty-seven month commitment and the lack of choice in your destination.

There are, however, many other volunteer groups that have much shorter term opportunities available. The only catch with many of these other organizations is that there are quite often (in fact, *most* often) significant fees involved. When I first looked into volunteering, I couldn't understand why I would have to pay a fee to volunteer. After all, I have a wide array of skills, speak four languages, and am a hard worker. Why should I pay to volunteer? After I researched it further, I discovered that most of these organizations are funded primarily through volunteer contributions. That is how they get the money to pay their staff, conduct their research, and provide food, shelter and training for their volunteers.

There are many types of volunteer organizations. I have outlined some of the major organizations and provided some resources in the appendix. Briefly, there are volunteer organizations for:

- Working with wildlife

- Working at animal sanctuaries

- Working with children in indigenous communities

- Teaching English

- Working on ships or sailboats

- Participating in archeological research

- Building housing for the needy

- Working with doctors or medical personnel in remote locations

Truly, there is no shortage of opportunities to see the world while making a difference, the biggest difference being in your own self!

Schools: Language, Trade, or Sport

If volunteering is not your thing, there is always the chance to learn a new skill. Cooking schools, sailing schools, language immersion schools, and even trade schools abound overseas. Or perhaps you've wanted to learn to dive, horseback ride, mountain climb, or ski. Many specialized sporting schools exist as well. Just be sure when selecting a program that it will allow you plenty of time for meditation and reflection—the goal is *not* to fill up all of your waking hours. You will need several hours of downtime (at least three, not counting the evenings) per day for reflection. Without this, your trip or experience will be pointless.

Marie's Story

∞

Imagine for a moment that every day you care for people at the end of their lives. Your goal isn't always to cure them, but sometimes to ease their transition from this life to the next. Now imagine that your patients are not the elderly, but children with terminal illnesses.

Not only do many people regard your career choice with horror, but there are those within your own profession who view what you do with distaste, claiming that the palliative care approach is simply one of giving up when more aggressive strategies and treatments should be pursued. Your detractors don't take into account the pain and suffering experienced in protracted treatments, many of which are experimental and will have limited success. For these professionals, defeating disease is more important than the comfort and quality of life of each patient.

Doctors engaged in palliative care are not proponents of giving up. They simply want to make it possible for the families of these children to examine all choices, including the choice of going home to be with their loved ones, even if that means stopping treatment.

Marie (not her real name) worked in the intensive care unit of a hospital in a large metropolitan area on the East Coast. About seven years ago, a sixteen year old boy who was in need of an organ transplant was admitted to her unit. Week after week, month after month, she watched as the boy and his family both deteriorated: one physically, the other emotionally. It was too much for her. "I just felt that we somehow abandoned not the child, but the family. We could not come to grips with the fact that he was dying."

Marie decided to unplug, leaving her nursing career behind for a stint at cooking school. For the next six months, she focused her mind on the simple but backbreaking tasks involved in restaurant work: chopping vegetables and standing over hot stoves. It was such a total change from the emotionally draining work she was used to that it proved a cathartic experience. She realized she had a love for nursing, but knew something had to change. When she finished chef school, she returned to her career, but this time in palliative care.

Had Marie not taken the time to unplug from nursing, she may have eventually burned out completely. Today, she still works in the field she loves best, but has found a niche that better suits her empathic nature.

Nature vs. Nurture

When selecting the type of experience you are about to have, you will be faced with myriad choices. Perhaps you're an accountant who's secretly dreamed of becoming a chef—cooking school in Paris might appeal to you. Or perhaps you're a chef who's always dreamed of sailing around the world—you might be inclined to go to Miami to take boating lessons. Perhaps you are of Italian heritage and you'd like to finally learn to speak Italian fluently—a language school in Rome might seem right up your alley. Those may all seem to be good ideas, but…

Paris, Miami, and Rome are all cosmopolitan locations. You will hardly be able to unplug there. So, when I say a location foreign to you, the first and foremost criterion I am thinking of is that the location should be more natural than digital. Your daily surroundings should enable you to hear the sound of birds more than cars, of the ocean more than planes, or perhaps just plain silence.

That is not to say that your goal of chef school in Paris should be forgotten, just rethought or postponed. How about trying a school in a more rural region of France instead? Instead of language school in Rome, why not a location deep down in the heel of the boot, where English is still a rarity? Instead of Miami, why not take your boating lessons in Costa Rica? The key is to follow a buried passion while reconnecting to a more natural environment. If after a month or two of cooking school in the Pyrenees, Paris is still calling, you have really lost nothing. But in the meantime, you will have had the chance to get to know yourself without the hustle and bustle and distractions of city life.

A Further Option

The previous choices have all more or less been directed at those of you needing a break of at least three months, those who really need to get to know yourselves (perhaps for the first time). For those who are lucky enough to be relatively self realized, but just need time away from the system for reflection, healing, or both, I recommend a third choice—monasteries. (Before you skip over this section, believing that I am suggesting you become a monk or a nun, read on.) Monasteries are actually wonderful places for those seeking a shorter term break. They are often remote, surrounded by nature, and definitely devoid of the trappings of modern consumerism. Moreover, many of them are located in absolutely stunning locations, and welcome visitors.

I became aware of this option long after my sabbatical was concluded, on a plane from London to Phoenix. My seatmate appeared to be a nun, but she was dressed in a powder blue habit, unlike anything I'd seen before. My writer's curiosity forced me to ask her about it, and thus began an interesting conversation that lasted for several hours. She showed me pictures of her monastery in Monterrey, Mexico. It was a gorgeous structure, apparently still under construction, perched high on a cliff overlooking the ocean. When she learned that I speak Italian, she invited me out to the monastery to give lessons to the monks, in exchange for being able to stay there. My husband could join me too, she said. (Other opportunities to exchange a skill for a stay were possible.) She showed me more pictures, each depicting the nuns and monks in their brightly colored clothing, their happy countenances shining as they ate, drank, and worshipped in this stunning retreat by the sea.

Packing It In

Regardless of your destination, one condition is paramount —travel light! Whether you are headed to the mountains or the tropics, the last thing you need to do is burden yourself with more than you can comfortably carry. Even if you will be gone for six months or more, do not take more than one rolling suitcase and one carry-on bag.

Your carry-on should be large enough to stow all of your necessary prescriptions, papers, and an emergency change of clothes. As unrefined as this choice may seem, a backpack is really the best choice for a carry-on since it will leave your hands free to manage your other suitcase and navigate airports and train stations with greater ease. If both hands are tied up carrying luggage, it's much more difficult to fish for ID and tickets.

The key to traveling light is to think in layers and stick to basic color schemes, preferably neutrals. This type of journey should not involve haute couture. Rather, you want to be as comfortable, and as inconspicuous—especially if traveling internationally—as possible. Choose clothes that are lightweight and easy to clean and dry. This is obviously easier (and more important) when traveling to warmer climates rather than cold ones. See the appendix for recommended travel outfitters.

Possibly the most important consideration when packing will be your footwear. Comfort is crucial. If you will be in a remote area, you want to make absolutely certain that your feet are happy. You may have heard the expression, "If Mama ain't happy, ain't nobody happy." The same goes for your feet. Depending on the length of your journey, it may even be a good idea to pack two pairs of your favorite kinds of shoes, just to be on the safe side.

It is highly unlikely you will need more than half a dozen outfits, even if you will be gone long term. What you will need plenty of are undergarments. While you can wear the same shirt more than once without washing it, the same isn't true of socks or underwear.

A word about jeans—don't. While jeans are the utmost in comfort, they are not the best for travel. They take up a lot of room, and take forever to dry. I wore jeans on my first trip to Costa Rica. As I was walking to my hostel on the first day, it began to rain. Soon the rain was coming down so hard that it was ricocheting off of the pavement and drenching me from the bottom up. Not only did it take my jeans over two weeks to dry, but I eventually had to throw them away because of the mold that settled in them.

In terms of health precautions, the CDC's website has an excellent section on what to pack when traveling. (See the appendix for the link.) It's a good idea to create a checklist of what to pack as you are researching your destination. Rely on tips from other travelers, travel sites, and government agencies. Plan for a final inventory assessment no later than a week before your departure. You will be busy enough with last minute details—you don't need the additional stress of shopping for more items.

Summary

- A stay of at least three months is necessary for those on a true inner journey —six months to a year is ideal. For those just needing a refreshing break, two weeks to a month is ideal.

- Choose a location that limits your access to television, cell phones, and the Internet.

- Your destination should be a completely foreign environment: you *should* feel out of your element. This location needn't be out of the country.

- An organized group experience—whether through a volunteer organization or some type of school—will aid in reducing your anxiety.

- For those requiring a shorter break, a stint at a monastery can be just the ticket.

- For a full list of ideas, organizations, and options, see the appendix.

- Regardless of your destination, travel light. Be sensible and simple in your choices, and develop a customized checklist for your destination several weeks prior to your departure. Then check it twice, a week before leaving.

Small Steps to Freedom: Writing Exercise

Imagine that a travel genie has just popped out of a bottle. She is going to grant you an all expense paid trip to anywhere in the world you'd like to go, as long as you decide in one minute. Which destination would you name? Why? Why haven't you gone yet?

No matter how farfetched, or how extreme, this is the destination you should probably unplug to, with the exception of major cities.

Chapter Four

Dancing on the High Wire

Unplugging on Your Own

O KAY, SO YOU'VE DECIDED YOU'RE GOING TO DO it. You've revved up your courage, picked a destination, and notified your friends and family. Telling others is the first step to full commitment. This is partially due to the fact that you will spend so much time justifying your seemingly crazy decision that you will not change your mind easily from this point forward.

If you're like most people, you also have someone else you need to inform about your decision—your employer. What happens next will have a tremendous impact on your life from this point forward, so be sure to fully consider all of the implications of this chapter.

You basically have two choices: give notice and quit your job, or request some type of sanctioned leave of absence (such as a formal sabbatical). Even if you choose the latter, you could be facing a minefield, so an entire chapter has been devoted to this concept (see Chapter 5, "Unplugging with a Safety Net").

In this chapter, we'll be discussing how to unplug on your own: when to give notice, how to give notice, and what to expect. You will learn from the mistakes of others and hopefully find the best approach for your unique situation.

Why Walk the Wire?

Whether you choose to unplug on your own or take a sanctioned leave of absence should depend primarily on how much you actually enjoy what you currently do (irrespective of your current boss). Not everyone wishing to unplug is doing so because they dislike their career. If you generally enjoy what you do, but just need some time away for self development, then you should definitely consider researching your company's policy on leaves of absence. Keep in mind that even companies with fairly liberal policies will expect something from you in return—usually a commitment of at least one year. If you love what you do, great! If you hate it, your time away will pretty much be in vain since the entire experience will be clouded by your impending return to something you are dreading.

Take This Job

If you've decided that you'd like to sing along with Johnny Paycheck, you need to be very careful about how you actually do it. In fact, no matter how much you dislike your present employer, it's *not* advisable to tell your boss to "take this job and shove it." More realistically, you need to decide how you're going to give notice, and how much notice to give.

The goal here is to leave on the best possible terms without compromising your own financial security. It is advisable not to give notice unless and until you are in a financial position to do so. Depending on your relationship with your boss, the relative uniqueness of your duties and talents, and even the mood your boss wakes up in that day, you could find yourself suddenly not having to report to work the next day. Make sure that when that moment comes, you are ready to meet your obligations and still embark on your journey with a reduced level of stress.

Some people, myself included, feel comfortable giving one month (or more) notice. While this has the potential to work out for some people, it's definitely a more than generous amount of time to give. For me, the main reason for giving so much notice was to make myself follow through on my promise to unplug. Once I gave notice, there was really no going back. I also have the habit of staying on very good terms with my employers, because you never know when you might just need that glowing reference.

You should feel comfortable giving more than the standard two weeks notice if:

- Your boss has no idea how to produce the same output as you

- You don't have a coworker who has similar skills and responsibilities

- The work your department produces is vital to the company's day-to-day operations

That last one is pretty important. One manager gave her company more than two months notice since she was managing an entire department, only to find that the company never actually replaced her. It seemed that the department could not only function perfectly well without her, but their output went generally unnoticed by the rest of the company as well. Fortunately for her, none of this was observed until well after she had embarked on her journey, otherwise she may have even been laid off immediately after giving her notice.

How you give notice is just as important as how much notice you give. The best course is to craft a positive, well reasoned letter to your boss. Being able to hand your boss something in writing prevents you from saying the wrong thing under stress. Make no mistake—no matter how happy you are to be leaving your job, the experience is going to be tinged with self doubt, fear and insecurity. After all, you are not running into the arms of a waiting employer. Rather, you are setting off on a journey for which you don't really know the final destination.

What you say in this letter is also very important. The main thing is to keep it short, sweet and firm. Don't profess how unhappy you are in your current position. You never know—this could change once you've had the shift in perspective that only time and distance can allow. Do state how grateful you are for the opportunities you've been afforded. Don't leave it open to discussion. Do set a firm date for departing. Don't mention that you are going on a personal journey; this could be seen as flaky by closed minded people (of which the world has plenty). Do say that you have decided to take advantage of a personal opportunity. If you will be engaging in some volunteer work (as discussed in the next section) feel free to mention it. If you have no firm plans, then the less said, the better. Do offer to recruit and train your replacement, and to be available for questions for a limited time. Don't give the impression that you feel you are irreplaceable.

Keep in mind that it is important to stay on good terms with your employer, if for no other reason than your next employer will likely contact them before hiring you. Therefore, never give less than two weeks notice. It is unprofessional and discourteous, and will only come back to haunt you. If your employer chooses to let you go before the two weeks expire, that's their choice.

Minding the Gap

What you say to your employer may resurface (or come back to haunt you) later on. If you are doing a proper unplugging (one month to one year), then you will have a gap on your résumé that you will need to explain to your future employer. If you leave on bad terms, there is a strong possibility that when your future employer contacts your last employer for a reference, they may hear that you are unreliable or not a good risk. This can happen regardless of what your former employer actually *says*—it's more a matter of what is *not* said. This is why leaving on good terms is of paramount importance. It needs to be absolutely clear to your future employer that leaving was your own choice.

Why Volunteering Is Key

If you unplug as part of a corporate sponsored sabbatical, no explanation to future employers will be necessary. In fact, assuming you fulfill your obligation to said employer and continue to work there upon your return, no gap will even be present on your résumé.

However, if you decide to quit your job and fly solo, you need to be sure that this time is not later viewed as a temporary lapse of reason and responsibility. The best way to do this is to volunteer. Including time on a volunteer project will fulfill several key aspects of your inward journey.

- You can try out a career that you've always dreamed of, without first investing in the additional education, materials and resources. For example, if you think you'd like to teach children, volunteer with an indigenous community. If you think you would like to work with animals, volunteer on a wildlife preserve. If you think you'd like to go into medicine, volunteer for Hospice or at a hospital. There are several volunteer organizations listed in the appendix, as well as portals to many more.

- Volunteering takes the pressure and focus off of you and your current situation. By knowing that you are actively involved in making the lives of others better, much of what you are artificially attached to will fall away, without conscious effort on your part. You will find yourself refreshed and revitalized.

- Volunteering will allow you to make several connections, both with other like minded volunteers and with the organizations you are volunteering for. Many organizations, such as Global Vision International, give preference and priority for job openings to those who have volunteered with them. In case your dream career does in fact turn out to be a good fit, you'll already have one foot in the door.

- Volunteering looks good on a résumé. Telling a future employer that you took some time off to work with communities affected by a hurricane or a tsunami will cast a far more favorable light on you than saying, "I took some time off to find myself."

Forging Alliances

Since you have no way of knowing whether your journey will result in a new career or a return to your present situation, it is vital to be prepared for both. You should be aware that even giving generous notice and doing everything by the book may not result in good feelings with your immediate supervisor. There are several reasons for this. The most obvious is one of pure envy—not everyone has the courage and spirit to see something like this through. Your boss may never tell you, but it's likely that he wishes he could do what you are doing, rather than being saddled with additional responsibility. The second reason is also common: your departure, no matter how well planned, places a burden on your boss's shoulders. They must hire and train a new person to fill your shoes, which can be difficult. Also, the timing that may be best for you could be the worst for the company. While you should definitely not let this deter you, you should also be aware of the implications. Finally, your boss may feel personally betrayed by your decision, which is more likely if the two of you have developed a strong rapport and good working relationship.

What this ultimately means is that you should be sure to have someone else on your side. Realistically, this should be someone other than a peer, who will not only have many of the same objections as your boss, but also isn't as impressive a reference. The best potential references are end users of some type, whether they report directly to you or are a higher ranking internal client. If the nature of your job doesn't include internal clients, it's still beneficial to list a higher ranking employee who is familiar with (and impressed by) you and your work.

It is also important to understand that these types of relationships cannot possibly be forged overnight. So, if you have not already expended the energy to form these relationships, it may be too late, depending of course on how quickly you plan to give notice. If your departure is imminent, just keep these factors in mind when thinking of whom to list as a reference. If you have several months before giving notice, it wouldn't hurt to start finding some commonalities with these types of people now.

Put Me in Coach!

Speaking of having someone on your side, you may consider hiring a personal lifestyle coach. There are two major differences between mentors and coaches. A mentor is someone, usually in your own field or profession, who counsels you and dispenses advice based on her own experience. A coach is a paid professional trained to help you reach new levels of growth, drawing from *your* personal and professional experiences. The difference is critical. If you are unplugging on a corporate sponsored sabbatical as discussed in the next chapter, you most likely will be in need of a mentor. If you are unplugging on your own and wish to create a totally new life, you'll most likely need the services of a coach.

The main challenge associated with hiring a coach is the expense—expect to pay several hundred dollars per consultation. You'll most likely get what you pay for: unbiased, useful advice from a trained professional which will serve you well in your future endeavors. However, when you consider the expense involved in financing your journey while meeting your existing obligations, this may not prove a viable option for you. On the other hand, some individuals who hire coaches find their need to go on an extended journey diminished or eliminated, and simply use the knowledge gained to transform their lives without unplugging. I won't blame you for wondering, "Where's the fun in that?" The truth is that achieving a life transformation without unplugging is certainly possible, but expect it to take longer and to be significantly more difficult. Unplugging allows you to shut out most of your distractions and detractors. It's far easier to reach the summit of your dreams when you are climbing the mountain with a single focus.

This book was designed to provide you with a portion of the coaching you need to pursue your dreams. If you can afford to also hire a coach, by all means do so! (See the appendix for information on how to find a coach.)

Clive's Story

∞

To the outside world, it appeared that the thirty-three year old software marketing executive had achieved it all: a master's degree from Cambridge, a six figure income, a house in the country, and a wife. He also had a company car and stock options, and was living a debt free life. Virtually every item on Life's List of Success had been checked off.

What wasn't outwardly apparent was Clive's inner world: "Under the surface of my outwardly successful life, there were signs that I was killing myself. I smoked and drank too much. I felt angry and stressed at work. Many of the people who worked for me were afraid of my temper."

Although Clive had already taken several sabbaticals in the past, including a backpacking trip across Asia and diving trips on Australia's Great Barrier Reef, he still hadn't managed to connect to himself.

In 1997, he had a spiritual awakening in response to an inner voice that told him, "This day is the turning point in your life." Clive decided to trust this inner voice and prepare for his next sabbatical—one which would have an inner focus rather than just be another adventure. "I went to study in a Shree Muktananda Ashram, eventually spending five years studying and serving the mission. There I helped hundreds of people take extended breaks from their careers to visit the ashram for two to twelve month periods." As a result, Clive also discovered his next career as a coach.

Today, Clive is one of the top 1600 executive life coaches accredited by the International Coach Federation as a Professional Certified Coach (PCC). He lives with his wife Abigail (also a coach) and new daughter Iona in one of the most beautiful places in the world—the San Juan Islands in Washington State. Most importantly, he has re-centered his life around his own family, working just two to three days a week. "This gives us plenty of time to play, learn, and grow together." Clive's coaching business is featured under "Coaching" in the appendix.

Summary

- When deciding how much notice to give, consider the uniqueness of your work, the skills of your coworkers and boss, and the relative importance of what you produce to the company overall.

- How you give notice is just as important as how much notice you give. Written notice in the form of a well reasoned letter will prevent you from saying the wrong things under pressure. Keep your letter short, sweet, and firm.

- Mind the gap—be sure you can explain the gap on your résumé adequately to future employers. Know what you will say before you quit.

- Consider volunteering. It's a great way to try out a new career, as well as take the focus off of yourself for a while. Not only does volunteering look better on a résumé than unexplained time off, but it could also eventually lead to your dream job.

- Forge alliances. Regardless of how well you handle leaving your current employer, it is likely that your boss and coworkers will feel some level of resentment upon your departure. Try to build relationships and find commonalities with those above and below you who are familiar with and benefit from your output. These types of people make the best references.

- Consider hiring a personal lifestyle coach to aid with your goal setting. The right coach can even help shorten the length of your journey. For those for whom going on a journey is truly impossible (for example, the care-taker of an ill or elderly parent), hiring a professional coach may even eliminate the need to travel at all.

Small Steps to Freedom: Writing Exercise

Who would be the first person you would tell about your decision to unplug? What do you imagine their reaction might be? Is it important to you for this person to react a certain way to your news?

How do you feel when you imagine yourself giving notice to your employer? Is it important for your current employer to be okay with your decision? Why or why not?

Craft a paragraph explaining your time away to a future employer.

Chapter Five

Unplugging with a Safety Net
The Corporate Sabbatical

I F YOU ARE FORTUNATE ENOUGH TO WORK FOR A
forward thinking company, you may have the option of
a corporate sponsored sabbatical. As mentioned in the
previous chapter, this option is best for those who are not
necessarily seeking a career change, but rather need to unplug
for different reasons. Examples include getting over a failed
relationship, pursuing spiritual growth, or engaging in other
aspects of personal development.

According to the Society for Human Resource Management, the percentage of companies offering some type of sabbatical is growing. Their most recent study shows that roughly
11 percent of large companies offer paid sabbaticals, while 29
percent offer unpaid leave. In addition, 16 percent of small
companies and nearly a quarter of mid-size companies offer
unpaid sabbaticals. The larger the corporation, the greater

the chance the sabbatical includes some form of pay—usually 50 percent, as well as continued benefits coverage.

You might very well be wondering, "Why are companies offering sabbaticals to their employees at all?" The answers are varied:

- It's an innovative way to attract and retain employees, without a significant cash outlay.

- Employees come back feeling energized and, most importantly, grateful. Gratitude breeds loyalty.

- The employees filling in for their supervisors or coworkers on sabbatical have a chance to expand their skills.

- Sabbaticals foster increased creativity upon the employee's return to work.

The fact that major corporations such as Intel, Microsoft, Nike, American Express, and Proctor and Gamble offer sabbaticals illustrates the fact that sabbaticals can be good for a company's bottom line, so don't be afraid to ask for one if it's offered.

On the flip side, human resource directors do admit that making sabbaticals available to their employees requires a great deal of planning. Usually, the employee must coordinate her leave at a time that is convenient for the company (i.e. not during a major advertising campaign or new product launch). At a large corporation, this could mean coordinating the schedules of several hundred employees, as well as making sure their duties are covered. While it's entirely possible that your employer will grant you a leave of absence, keep in mind that the experience may not be 100 percent on your terms.

Begin with the End in Mind

Before you even set foot out the door, you need to have a re-entry strategy. The most difficult thing about going on a defined corporate sabbatical is the shock of coming back. So if you are allowed eight weeks, be sure you return home no later than day one of week seven. You will need some adjustment time to catch up on bills and correspondence and confront personal landmines before you will be able to handle professional challenges.

Ideally, your first day back at work should also fall towards the middle of the week, such as on a Wednesday, to allow you to ease back into the nine to five paradigm. Going back to work on Monday after several weeks off will make your first week at work last an eternity.

Plan a homecoming party with your closest friends and family prior to starting work, and set the date *before* you depart. Ask a friend to be in charge of reminding everyone about it. For simplicity, make it a potluck. This will be your time to share photos and stories from your adventures, and hand out the trinkets and souvenirs you may have acquired. This may strike you as an odd piece of advice, but the truth is that you will be bursting to share your experiences, insights, and revelations with anyone who will listen. It's best if you get this out of your system before you show up to work—these stories are most appropriate for (and most appreciated by) members of your support network. As soon as you show up to work, make sure you are 100 percent there, ready to check your freewheeling sabbatical-taking persona at the door.

Build Your Case

Most companies offering sabbaticals have some type of hierarchy in place when it comes to granting them. While a company's only *stated* requirement may be the length of time you have been employed, the reality of the decision making process may be a bit more convoluted.

Corporations are unlikely to grant sabbaticals to poor performers; an exception could be a previously top performer who has experienced some personal setbacks. In this case, the employer might even be pushing you to take advantage of their program, with the hope of garnering a significant return on their investment. Likewise, those who are not viewed as team players will also find their chances greatly diminished.

If you are thinking about applying for a corporate sabbatical, there are several factors you should keep in mind:

- It's never too early to start planning to apply. Ideally, you should allow at least three months of personal and professional preparation before you even approach your boss. (While each company's deadlines for granting leaves of absence will differ, this is a reasonable benchmark for most individuals considering a sabbatical.) It will allow sufficient time to alter existing perceptions about you and your work product, if necessary, as well as give you ample time to ensure this is something you really want. The last thing you want to do is apply for a program of this nature, and then change your mind. Needless to say, this will create unfavorable impressions regarding your stability, and make it less likely that a future request will be considered seriously.

- Share your decision with a mentor. Ideally, your mentor is not someone you report to, nor who would have a conflict of interest. Your mentor should be someone familiar with you in a professional capacity who can provide you with guidance regarding growth areas that need to be addressed. This person should also be someone you trust who has nothing to gain from competing with you professionally. Therefore, it is highly unlikely that your mentor will be a coworker or a peer. Keep in mind that your mentor needn't work for the same company you do, but should be in a related field, or have direct knowledge of your company. Choose a mentor who will be familiar with both your company's ideology as well as your own potential areas for growth.

- Keep it professional. Are you currently besieged with personal calls and email while at work? Do you come in looking tired due to lack of sleep? Has your personal appearance or grooming suffered? Are you tardy? For the next three months, make a conscious and concerted effort to address these types of issues. Investing more time in your professionalism and work ethic today will not only pay off tomorrow, but also while you are enjoying your corporate sponsored sabbatical many months from now.

- Improve your product. Since you're reading this book, chances are good that you are looking forward to some time off. It's also possible that your work product isn't as complete or perfect as it once was. This is the time for some critical self-evaluation: is your performance truly up to par? Make a list of things you feel need improvement, then start improving them! Start with the simplest things and check them off as you go. This will build your sense of confidence and fuel your desire to improve, making each successive task easier. Conversely, if you start with the most difficult task, you will feel discouraged and end up accomplishing nothing.

- Become a true team member. This is perhaps the most critical piece of advice for this preparatory period. You could be the most efficient, professional, and productive employee in the company, but if you are not visible, none of that will matter. Think about it. Pretend you are on the committee reviewing applications for sabbaticals. On the one hand, you have Mary, who is a hard worker, shows up on time, has never missed a day and is consistent in her workload. She also never interacts with other employees, preferring to keep to herself entirely. On the other, you have John, who is a fairly good employee in terms of work product and professionalism, but also volunteered for the recent quality initiative, organized prizes for the company golf tournament, and always seems to be the one passing out cards for someone's birthday or get well wishes. Who would *you* choose to reward? This is not to say that you must undergo a complete personality transplant. Rather, think of this as your time to be noticed. Once you are noticed, it is far more likely that you have the potential to be missed when you are gone. Obviously, companies would much rather reward employees they like with a sabbatical, whereas they may just be glad to see a surly person leave—permanently.

- Know that you will likely only have one shot. Don't try to take any shortcuts. If you apply for a sabbatical and fail, this could end up causing you to feel resentful and negative, which will be very difficult to mask. While there are no guarantees that following these suggestions will result in your application being granted, doing so will definitely increase your chances.

Apply with Grace

If you've followed the above suggestions and are at the end of your three month preparation period, you are now ready to apply. The biggest question is: are you still ready to do this?

Perhaps now that you've tightened the reins on your professionalism and become more of a team member, you might find yourself looking forward to going to work and are not as desirous of a sabbatical. Alternatively, the situation causing you to want to unplug may have resolved itself and you no longer wish to embark on your journey. If this is the case, don't be afraid to admit it to yourself. After all, you've lost nothing.

If, on the other hand, you find yourself ready and desirous of a break, the time has (finally) come. You've spent the last three months molding yourself into a perfect employee, one who deserves to be rewarded. Make sure these were not wasted efforts. How you apply is also very important.

Your first step should be to read your company's policy manual, if you have not already done so. Many companies have instituted online searchable databases containing information on benefits and procedures. Doing your research before approaching your boss and Human Resources would be a wise idea.

Whom you approach first—your boss or the HR department—will depend on your relationship with your boss. If you have a comfortable relationship with your boss, by all means approach her first. Here are some tips to keep in mind when making that first approach.

- Avoid drama. It may be tempting to stagger into your boss's office looking distraught and pleading for the time off. Don't! The main message you need to communicate is that this is a reasonable request that has been well thought out and considered. You also should communicate that your job is important to you, and you feel that taking this time off will benefit both you and the company.

- Have your paperwork accessible. While it shouldn't be completely filled out, you should demonstrate that you have taken the initiative to research the matter and are not asking on a whim. Your boss may wish to look it over, so it would be a good idea to have important sections highlighted or tabbed.

- Show consideration for how your plan will affect your boss and coworkers. Prepare a written outline of your existing duties, and who in your opinion could help with your tasks. Make it clear these are only suggestions—you do not want to be perceived as arrogant. For example, you could say, "Since Mandy is already familiar with Access, it would be relatively easy for me to train her to run my weekly status report." Show that you are ready to step up to the plate when it comes to training others on how to perform your duties.

- Be flexible with your timing. Let your boss know that you understand that your decision will impact him as well as the company. Ask him up front when he thinks the best time would be for you to depart. Although it's pretty likely that your boss and HR department will have the final say anyway, the fact that you are taking his own issues into consideration will reflect favorably on you as a team player.

- Craft an inspiring mission statement. When it comes to filling out the paperwork, be prepared to name at least one personal goal you hope to attain during your sabbatical. Make sure this goal, although personal in nature, will also provide an obvious benefit to the company. For example, if you will be working as a volunteer home builder in a disaster stricken community, you could write, "I will be working on expanding my team building skills while working with the victims of

Hurricane Katrina." The important thing is to find an angle that shows some benefit to the company. Even if you're a marketing executive going off to chef school, you can still craft a pithy mission statement. "I will be recharging my creativity by learning new skills in a relaxing environment. I hope to come back with a fresh perspective and lots of new ideas." This mission statement will be very important—not only will it win you the approval of your boss, it can also affect how your peers and coworkers perceive of you. Stating a clear goal and purpose for your time away will help mitigate feelings of envy or resentment from your coworkers, ensuring a smoother return.

- Set expectations regarding communication while you are gone. While a true sabbatical should involve no communication between employer and employee, this can vary within each firm. Allow some "panic time" after your last day in the office for your boss and coworkers to contact you with unforeseen questions. In other words, don't depart for Timbuktu the next day. Ideally, you want several days of transition time between your departure from the office and becoming truly unplugged. When that time comes, don't be reachable! Leave a number in case of emergency, but even if your cell phone actually works, don't let anyone know this. (Better yet, leave it at home.) You will not be truly unplugged if you are constantly anticipating being contacted by your former life. If your boss insists on a compromise, arrange to call in or check email at predetermined intervals (no more frequently than twice a month).

Keep the Best and Forget the Rest

We've already discussed the importance of reintegrating slowly back into your work schedule at the conclusion of your sabbatical. The key word here is *integration*. Be sure that upon returning, you will incorporate one or more aspects of your time off into your new daily routine. It will be impossible for you to know in advance what this will include, but make a promise to yourself to remember to do this. Program a reminder into a utility such as Outlook before you leave, or leave yourself a note in a prominent place at home. It can be a simple note such as "What will I miss?"

Personally, I did several things to keep the spirit of my journey alive. For example, I had several of my favorite photographs of wildlife and natural scenery turned into posters and hung them in my office. Every time I look at them I am reminded of my great adventure and of the happiness I felt. Since I also enjoyed the part of my time off spent teaching, I decided to apply as an adjunct instructor for several online universities. While I haven't changed careers, I still stay active doing something I love.

Perhaps your work with an environmental organization will inspire you to join Greenpeace or the Sierra Club, or to start a recycling program at the office. Alternatively, you may decide to volunteer one weekend a month in your local park. The goal is to do something related to what you most enjoyed while on sabbatical, in order to keep those positive associations alive. Doing this will prevent early burnout. Just be careful not to overload your schedule.

The most common complaint from those returning from a sabbatical is that they can't wait until their next one. While you will certainly have an excellent grasp on what it takes to embark on such a journey now that you have returned from one, it would be wise to keep these thoughts to yourself—at least until you become eligible again. For most companies, this is upwards of seven years.

Expect the Unexpected

Since most organizations are somewhat fluid in nature, be prepared to face the fact that you might not be returning to exactly the same position you had when you left. Obviously, this depends on how long you were gone. Before you panic, this is not to say that you will not have a job when you return. In fact, you will very likely still have the same position, title, and salary as you did when you left. However, some things are bound to have changed. Remember Mandy and her knowledge of Access? She may have decided that running one additional report would be no problem at all for her, permanently. Or, she may have discovered that she already produces a report that covers the same information. Consequently, both of your workloads may have been lightened. (It's amazing how quickly the average employee can transform into the most scrupulous efficiency expert when saddled with additional responsibility.)

Also, be prepared for the fact that the company may have undergone its own changes, which had nothing to do with you or your time away. You may have worked for the same boss for ten years but come back to find a new face sitting in the corner office. While it's tempting to think that we are hitting a giant "pause" button on the rest of the world while we go off to evolve and find ourselves, this is hardly the case. Consider this your reality check.

Obviously, the changes can impact you both favorably as well as negatively. You may find yourself slightly dreading the same old routine, only to find a completely new (and pleasant) environment upon your return. Or, you could be as lucky as Matt (see Chapter 10) and come back to find a promotion awaits you. Just remember to keep an open mind.

While most of you reading this chapter fully intend to return to the job you are leaving behind, it's entirely possible that you will experience a major transformation while you are gone. Time and distance work wonders on perspective, whether dealing with your career, your personal development, or your relationships. That's the whole point of getting unplugged.

If you should discover a new passion while on sabbatical that you'd like to devote your professional life to, great! But keep mum for now. Chances are good that you will have some sort of obligation to your employer on the other side of your sabbatical, whether it's six months or a year. If this is the case, do not share your desire to part with your employer immediately upon returning. Since changing careers (and possibly locations) is a time consuming endeavor anyway, just view this period of obligation as a paid transition period. Rather than being resentful of having to return to your old job, be thankful you will have a steady paycheck as you plan your new life. You should also be grateful that you had the courage to embark upon this life changing experience, when you could have spent the rest of your professional life doing something that didn't satisfy you as much as you thought it did.

Jon and Melanie's Story

∽

When Melanie decided to take advantage of her employer's sabbatical benefit, it was hardly the first time she had ever unplugged. On her own, she'd already traveled to a wide assortment of places, including a backpacking trip through Europe, a season in South America, and even a stint at the South Pole. The reason for her willingness to travel and open herself up to new experiences was a simple one: she was the daughter of parents from the hippie generation. "I guess you could say I was a flower child," she says.

When Melanie turned six, her father was hit by the financial reality of needing to support a family. He went back to school for a graduate degree, which landed him a job with the state of Oregon. He was able to provide his family a middle class lifestyle in a very conservative town. "It was a bit of a culture shock for us all, but within the walls of home we always talked about the importance of being true to oneself, which didn't come from material objects but experiences and relationships."

Ever since that time, she has tried to live her life with no regrets. "I have managed to unplug regularly throughout my life to ensure I am still on track, instead of because I am in crisis mode. I see it as regular, ongoing maintenance."

After graduate school, she began working for a Fortune 500 company and also met her future husband around the same time. When she was offered an expatriate position in Malaysia six months later, her husband was the first to sign them up. He had not traveled as much as she had, and was very excited about the chance to live abroad. "We moved to Malaysia a week after our wedding and lived there for one and a half years together. We took every opportunity we had (we had many 4 day weekends off) to travel and explore Southeast Asia."

JON AND MELANIE'S STORY, *cont.*

During this time, Jon was not working, so he took on the role of maintaining balance in their lives. Melanie was very excited about testing and challenging herself in her new career, and he had had a career for ten years and was ready to check out. So the couple easily adjusted to their new lifestyle. "Jon spent his days doing yoga, volunteering at an Indian restaurant, planning our travels, and taking care of my needs. It was a great life." After Malaysia, they accepted another short term assignment to Ireland, and then decided to repatriate. The decision was inspired by the long Irish winters as well as their desire to start a family.

In June of 2000 the couple moved back to Oregon and had their first child in August of that year. Melanie took four months off from work and Jon committed to being the stay-at-home parent when she went back to work, since he wasn't really employable at that point. "Talk about unplugging.... I felt like life slowed down to a crawl. Life doesn't get any more basic than when you are taking care of a newborn. I look back on those months with envy when I think about how simple life was—sleep, eat, change diaper—for four months."

When Melanie returned to work, Jon continued to keep balance in their lives and ensure not only that their child was well taken care of, but that dinner and the household chores continued to get done. "At this point, I still enjoyed my work. However, the main purpose of work became to provide for our family, and to allow one parent to remain at home with our child. Work was no longer a place to feed my soul."

The family welcomed a second child a year and a half later, and Melanie was able to take another four months off from work.

"During this time of child rearing, we were still reintegrating ourselves into the American ways. I continued to be overwhelmed by the number of choices in the grocery store and the big shiny cars that filled the street. We bought a modest home (a 1,100 square foot, 1910 bungalow) that we fixed up and we put in a wood stove that became our main heating supply. Since we were all consumed by figuring out how to be parents, it was a bit easier to hold off the pressures of the outside world from entering our home."

As their children grew older (they are now five and seven), the couple found it more and more difficult to do things on their own terms. "The children are influenced by their friends at school, TV, shopping malls, etc. Materialism and technology are everywhere. I find it more and more difficult to protect them from the material and fast paced life that is out there. My worst nightmare is that they are going to get sucked up in it all; however, I also don't want to shelter them from it. So, my dilemma is less about losing myself and more about losing my children."

In her seventh year at the company, Melanie was offered a chance to take a sabbatical. The family saw it as another opportunity to go on an adventure, but also to reinforce with their children the need to unplug periodically. "The timing was great because I was ready to check out again and was looking forward to not having to change diapers during my time away from work. Also, the children were only

JON AND MELANIE'S STORY, *cont.*

in preschool and kindergarten so it was not difficult pulling them out of school for two months." At this point, Jon had also decided he wanted to start his own business because the monotony of home life was getting to him. He was finally ready to re-enter the world after a seven year break.

The couple traveled to Baja, Mexico for two months. "For us, two months actually felt like a pretty short trip and because of our past travel experiences, a trip to Baja felt quite mild compared to some of the adventures we had experienced in the past." The difference, however, was that it was the first time they were adventuring with children. "I did question our judgment the first week camping on the beach when my husband lifted up the cooler and a three inch long scorpion ran out from underneath it. There was also the time we went to go swimming and there was a sea of sting rays in the water. My doubts were cleared when I saw how happy and content the children were playing in the sand and in the water and going to sleep under the stars each night. We slept in a tent for four weeks straight."

The family returned home a tighter, happier unit and Jon started a successful business. Melanie went back to work for her employer.

Unplugging regularly has become much more difficult as a family versus when they were a couple. "The daily demands are much greater, roots are deeper, and windows of opportunity are shorter," Melanie confides. Nonetheless, they give it their best shot. "Each summer, we take a two week road trip with the kids where we unplug as a family. We have been to Glacier,

Yellowstone, the Grand Tetons, and Telluride. This summer we are planning a trip to Whistler in BC."

On a day-to-day basis, Melanie admits that Jon is much better at staying in touch with himself than she is. "Even with a very successful business, he is religious about taking every Friday off from work to go fishing. The day is his time to unplug, be with nature, and clear his head. At first, I was quite resentful because it felt unfair that he had so much time to himself. Over the years, I have learned to respect the time and his ability to carve out this unplugged time on a regular basis." Melanie recently left the Fortune 500 company she worked for in order to follow her husband's example. "I am carving out the morning time as my own and I am attending yoga class twice a week."

Summary

- Begin with the end in mind. Craft a re-entry strategy that will ease you back into your routine.

- Build your case by improving your product, performance, and professionalism.

- Join the team. To make sure your efforts count, plan to become more visible. Companies most value those employees they know are there.

- Don't go it alone. Find a mentor to help you prepare for this major life change. This should not be a coworker, peer, or your boss. It should also not be someone with conflicts of interest between you and your employer.

- When applying, avoid drama. Make your request appear well reasoned and thought out.

- Be flexible with your timing. Show consideration for how your plan will affect others, especially your boss and coworkers, who will be picking up your slack.

- Create an inspiring mission statement and stick to it before, during, and after your journey.

- Set expectations regarding communications while away well before you depart. Allow some panic time between your last day in the office and the time of your departure.

- Upon your return, keep the best and forget the rest. Make sure you integrate aspects of your time away into your routine in order to keep the feeling of the sabbatical alive.

- Expect the unexpected. Be prepared to come back to a work environment that has also evolved. You may find yourself facing a new boss, new responsibilities, and a new routine.

- If your time away results in the desire for a new career, keep quiet about it upon your return. View your commitment to your current employer as a paid transition time that will help pave the way to a new, more rewarding, life!

- Don't be afraid of taking advantage of a paid sabbatical just because you have a family. You might be surprised at how powerful this bonding experience will be for your family. It is also an excellent opportunity to instill your own values in your children without the daily distractions and challenges they face at school and from other children.

Small Steps to Freedom: Writing Exercise

Think of someone you respect and admire within your profession. Write this person a letter (you won't be sending it) asking them to be your mentor, and the reasons you've chosen them.

List three goals you'd like your mentor to help you achieve as a result of this sabbatical.

Chapter Six

Show Me the Money
How to Pay for Your Adventure

SINCE THIS BOOK IS NOT NECESSARILY AIMED AT THOSE just graduating from high school or college, or those in retirement, it is likely you are tied down by things such as car and house payments, a lease on an apartment, debt, pets, and perhaps even a relationship. Thus, the first realization must be one of delayed gratification. In our pushbutton society, this is perhaps the second most difficult concept proposed in this book (the first one being the elimination of television, cell phones, and the Internet proposed in the previous chapters).

Naturally, the amount of money you must raise will depend on the length of your journey, and whether you are dancing on the high wire or unplugging with a safety net. One month is easily doable for most people. In fact, in many cases your employer may even grant you the time off. But as I've mentioned before, anything less than three months in duration is a waste of time for all but those who just need a refresher break. For those on a true inner journey, three months is the bare minimum, six months to a year is ideal. Therefore, you will need to invest some serious thought and financial planning in your adventure. The amount of debt you have, your current living arrangements, and your current satisfaction with your job are all factors that must be considered. They will also affect how much in advance you will need to plan your adventure.

Debt and Bills

The very first thing you will need to look at is the amount of debt you currently have. While it is not necessary to be completely debt free before embarking on your journey, the last thing you want is to be kept awake at nights by visions of mounting bills. At the very minimum, you need to be sure your monthly obligations are met in your absence. At best, you will eliminate or minimize these obligations as much as possible prior to your departure. For some of you, the amount of debt you have would mean having to postpone this journey for years, if not indefinitely. Given that, you will have some hard choices to make ahead.

The first step is to sit down and start recording your monthly expenses. Kudos if you already use some type of bookkeeping system or budget. You want to be sure to capture not only your monthly obligations (i.e. car payments, rent, mortgage, credit card bills) but also your discretionary spending. The latter is really the hardest to capture. One of the people in the case studies decided to track his spending by using a specific credit card for every purchase during a one month period. This gave him a paper trail for every single purchase. While I would suggest using a debit card instead, I thought this was a very good idea. If you prefer not to do that, then buy a small notebook (3x5) to carry with you, and be sure to record *all* of your purchases in it for a month. This will give you an idea of how much money you could actually be saving instead of flushing down the drain (in the form of mocha lattes, perhaps?).

The first goal is to try to save the money that is spent frivolously, to see how fast that can accumulate. The easiest way to do this is to set up an automatic transfer to your savings account each month, or perhaps from each paycheck. For most people, that is far easier than transferring the money to savings once it's been in their hands. Even if this is a small amount, say $50 a month, in a year you will have $600 more towards your goal (not including interest earned).

The second goal is to develop a debt payoff strategy. The simplest one is a principle endorsed by most debt management companies. Let's say you have three credit cards: a department store credit card with $1,000 balance, a Master-Card with $5,000, and a Visa with $7,500. Most people simply make the minimum payment (or slightly more) for each of these cards each month, allowing the interest to accumulate on each one, allowing their total debt to increase exponentially over time. Instead, the better approach is to figure out how quickly you can pay off the department store credit card, while making the minimum payments on the other cards. Let's say that realistically speaking, you can actually afford to pay $300 a month on the department store card, while still making the minimum payments on the two other cards. In a little over three months, you can have that card paid off, and can then start applying that $300 extra to the next lower balance card. Again, depending on how long you have until your journey, you may be able to either pay off all of your outstanding debt or at least reduce it so that you will have minimal monthly payments to be concerned about in your absence.

Many financial advisors will tell you that this simple method is actually preferred to debt consolidation services.

Using a debt consolidator can actually damage your credit rating, so it should be a last resort to be used with caution. Another option is transferring balances to different, lower rate cards. The caveat here is to be wary of introductory interest rates that will shoot up after the first few months. If you do get an offer of 0 percent interest on transfers, make sure you read the small print. If you feel confident that you can pay off your balance within the introductory time period, say six months, go for it. The trick is not to charge *anything else* on this card during this time.

Housing Situation

The biggest question here is whether you own or rent. If you own, you will need to decide if selling is an option, or if you feel comfortable renting your space while you will be gone. There are professional agencies that will aid you in renting your home, collecting payments on your behalf, and keeping an eye on your property. This type of service is strongly recommended if you choose to rent out your home.

Alternatively, you can choose to have a friend or relative housesit for you during your travels. Think twice about selling your home: this is not a decision that should be made lightly. It is always possible that after your sabbatical you will realize just how much you actually enjoy and appreciate your current home, job, relationship, etc. —you just needed the space away from it to be able to see it. In that situation, it would be horrible to have to try to recapture what was lost, most likely at a higher price. On the other hand, if your time away allows you to see your current environment as a trap, you can always put your house on the market after your return.

Renters are in a somewhat easier position. Unless you have signed an extremely long-term lease, you should be able to make your trip coincide with the end of your lease. If not, you can look into subletting (as long as it doesn't violate your lease agreement), or a more informal arrangement with a friend or family member.

Some people have opted to leave their possessions in the care of a trusted friend or family member. If you do not feel comfortable doing this, there are numerous affordably priced long-term storage facilities.

Your Stuff

Speaking of your possessions, it's now time to take a very close look at your surroundings. Most of the things that are likely to be in your line of sight at this very moment are actually unnecessary to your existence. The analogy that comes to mind is colored sprinkles on a cake. A cake surely tastes better with the icing, but do those little sprinkles really add any flavor? Unless you are already a highly evolved specimen in the anti-consumerist movement, you are likely to be surrounded by sprinkles. Fortunately for you, most of the rest of the world is also easily seduced by their empty calories, and you can actually make quite a bit of money as you downsize.

EBay springs to mind as the world's foremost market for many of these items. Amazon.com also offers a resale marketplace for used books, CDs, and movies. Leaving the cyberspace markets aside, there are always consignment stores, flea markets, and good old fashioned yard sales.

Your next task is to take a complete inventory of everything in your house. Start a chart with three columns: "Keep," "Sell," and "Donate." You should start with the items that are in plain sight, asking, "Do I use this regularly?" or "Can this item be replaced at a later date?" Chances are, the items in plain sight do get used quite a bit, but some might not get used at all, like that exercise bike in the corner, or that expensive massage chair you thought would eliminate trips to the spa. Any item that is collecting dust, or that you are keeping for reasons you don't understand anymore, or that is a relic from a past relationship should be eliminated.

This can be an extremely difficult process, so engage in your review with caution. Let's say you have an extensive cookbook collection. As you take each book in your hand, ask yourself "Have I cooked anything from this book in the last year?" "Have I at least opened this book over the last year to look at it?" and "Can this book be replaced if I change my mind?" If the answer to the first two questions was "no," it's probably a great candidate for Amazon's marketplace. This technique will eliminate clutter and help fund your trip.

Once you have done this for one of your collections, go through the same process with your jewelry, art work, furniture, clothing, electronics, and kitchen gadgets. By the time you're ready to go, you might be able to pay off a sizeable chunk of debt with the proceeds from the sale of your sprinkles. It may take several months, but the feeling of not having to worry about your apartment, your possessions, and most importantly, your bills will be liberating in the extreme.

Fundraising

For those of you with more debt than you are likely to pay off prior to your travels, there is another solution. In addition to eliminating wasteful spending, starting to save, and paying down your debt, you can start a fundraising campaign. This is easiest to justify if you are embarking on a volunteer vacation, since the money you will be requesting will be for a cause other than your own enlightenment. In fact, many volunteer organizations are able to provide you with fundraising ideas and kits. Here are a few tips I've picked up through the years, both as a volunteer and in my last position with Global Vision International, a company that specializes in conservation and community volunteer placements around the world.

- Be proactive: give yourself a reasonable amount of time to achieve your goal. You should start your fundraising efforts as soon as you have decided on a date.

- Be positive: make your contributors understand that they are helping you to transform lives, not just yours but also those in the communities you will be impacting.

- Be persistent: don't give up if you don't hear back from a potential donor; follow up!

- Research and use your contacts: make a list of everyone you can think of—your friends, your friends' friends, your family, their friends, local businesses, local community organizations, etc. Then send your fundraising letter to all of them!

- Get creative and use your imagination: if you don't feel comfortable asking for outright donations, consider a marathon, other sporting event, or something involving your own skills. Perhaps you can get local businesses to donate some wine or food, and then host a tasting party where the attendees will pay a fee. Alternatively, there is always the traditional bake sale or hobby expo.

- Be organized: make sure that the money you obtain from your fundraising effort is immediately placed in your short term savings account, or used to pay down bills. Don't spend it!

- Keep your goals in sight: to keep yourself motivated despite a mountain of bills, make a daily visit to your destination on the web, read a book about the life you're aspiring to, or conduct other research on your destination. Watch adventure movies. If you are gearing up for an archeological volunteer vacation, watch *Tomb Raider*. If you are going to Africa, watch *Duma*. If you are going to Italy, host a Fellini movie night and offer up a mini lesson in Italian in exchange for a small contribution. The goal is to sustain the excitement for your upcoming adventure through a period when you will be faced with a strict budget and tough financial decisions. To be successful, you'll need to keep the payoff in sight.

- Get your facts straight: if you will be partaking in a volunteer vacation, make sure you thoroughly research the company you will be working for. If they are non-profit, find out if contributors can send money for your expenses directly to the company in exchange for a tax write-off. If they do not have nonprofit status, find out exactly where the money is going and what some of their achievements are.

- Never be afraid to ask: opportunity sometimes only knocks once. If you have the chance to make a speech or presentation to a large group, don't be afraid to mention your fundraising objectives.

Grants, Loans, and Scholarships

You could also consider taking out a loan to finance your vacation. I know of a few people who have taken that approach successfully. They figured out how much money they needed to finance their adventure, and then took out the loan just prior to their trip. Payments were then withdrawn automatically from a checking or savings account while they were gone. This approach works only if you have no other debt, and if you are reasonably sure that you will be gainfully employed or otherwise able to pay it back upon your return.

Other options include grants (the best option there is, since you don't have to pay them back) or scholarships. These options are often available to those contemplating career changes, or who want to do some type of research on their trip. There is an excellent series of books by Matthew Lesko on how to get money to pay for virtually anything. They are worth investigating.

Current Job

Finally, it is time to consider your current employment situation. It is up to you to assess whether you are in a position to request a sabbatical, how much paid or unpaid time off you have, and how much notice you should give if you intend to quit. If you are reasonably certain that your position is important to the company—especially to your boss—you may feel comfortable giving a two to three month notice. This way, you would not need to resort to subterfuge. It is also a good way to generate a feeling of goodwill within the company. The potential payback from this approach is that you may be able to return to the company as a paid consultant in the future (as I did) or perhaps even have another job waiting for you there upon your return.

Giving that much notice will make the trip more real and will solidify your commitment to the journey. Once I gave notice and began to plan my adventure openly, I felt as if a giant weight had been lifted off of my shoulders.

This will not work for everyone, however. I know a handful of people who attempted this approach, and it backfired. It is up to you to determine how easily you will be replaced, if your decision will make it uncomfortable for you to continue working there, or if you will be let go after giving notice. Only you can make the best assessment of your situation. You may have to plan and execute your plan in total secrecy, giving only the requisite two weeks notice. If so, be sure to allow yourself at least two weeks after your last day of work to finalize your plans and tie up loose ends prior to departing. There is always more to do and plan for than you will antici- pate. If you are counting on that last paycheck, you want it to hit your bank account prior to leaving the country. You really don't want to find out your last paycheck bounced when you are out of the country. (Yes, this can happen, even with a check from a Fortune 500 company!)

Summary

- To be sure you've calculated all of your monthly liv- ing expenses, both obligatory and discretionary, keep track of all expenditures for an entire month, either by charging everything to a debit card, or by writing down all purchases in a small notebook.

- Start a savings fund from money that you might have squandered otherwise.

- Implement a debt reduction plan by paying off your lowest balance credit cards first.

- Use refinancing and balance transfer offers wisely.

- If you choose to rent out your home, consider using the services of a property management company.

- Consider obtaining grants, scholarships, or outright donations to fund your trip.

- Sell or donate the possessions in your life that are oth- erwise gathering dust.

- Be careful about when and how you give notice to your current employer.

Small Steps to Freedom: Writing Exercise

Starting with the room you are currently in, identify the "sprinkles" on the "cake" of your life. Which items could you really do without? Draw three columns on a page, label them "Keep," "Sell," and "Donate," and try to categorize every item in the room into one of those three categories. When you are finished with one room, move on to the next.

Then, next to the items you could sell, list where you could sell them, and how much they would net. If you would keep an item, write down if you would store it at home, with a friend or family member, or put it in storage.

Consider starting on your journey by donating some of the items on your list now. You'll feel liberated.

Chapter Seven

Taking Care of Business
Managing Your Responsibilities from Afar

I F YOU ARE PLANNING ON BEING GONE FOR LONGER than a month, you will need to invest some thought into making sure your obligations are being met in your absence.

The first step is to make sure you have an accurate list of all of your bills. If you are the type to maintain monthly itemized spreadsheets or are enrolled in an automated bill pay system, great! You should start by printing out a full year of your bills and searching for anomalies. While you probably have a pretty good grasp of your monthly obligations, it's those sneaky quarterly, semiannual, and annual bills that have the potential to derail your money train.

The ideal situation is to plan adequately for your recurring expenses in advance, and arrange for automatic payments. If you choose to self manage your finances in this way, be sure you have a reasonable cushion in your account to cover anything you may have missed. Twenty percent of the total is a good estimate for a reserve account.

As covered in Chapter 6, the amount of money you will need depends largely on whether you are unplugging on your own or embarking on a corporate sabbatical. The above percentage refers only to the total amount you will need to cover bills while you're unplugged, it does not refer to the financial cushion you may require if you come back without a job.

Prepayments vs. Automatic Payments

Some things, such as your auto and heath insurance, can be paid in one lump sum rather than on a monthly basis. Other bills, such as your mortgage or credit card bills, can't. One traveler was chagrined to discover that despite sending in very large payments to his credit cards and mortgage company, he came home to face late fees, elevated finance charges, and a house nearing foreclosure. If you have any doubts about the prepayment structure of your obligations, call the creditor in question.

Insurance

When it comes to health and auto insurance, there are several factors to consider. First, make sure your health coverage extends overseas if you will be traveling internationally. The last thing you want to do is become ill in a foreign location and be unable to pay for treatment. If you find that your current insurer will not cover you during your journey, you should purchase travel medical insurance. As someone who has spent time in a Costa Rican hospital on an intravenous drip for—of all the imaginable illnesses in the world—a mutant form of conjunctivitis, I can assure you that the unforeseen is likely to strike. Be prepared.

As far as auto insurance, your needs depend on whether you will be leaving your car behind or using it for transportation. If you're driving to the mountains of Montana, you'll obviously need full insurance. If you're headed out of the country and your car will be stored somewhere for several months to a year, be sure to let your insurance company know. Not only will they need the new location of your vehicle, but the fact that you won't be driving it may drastically reduce your rate.

Another factor to consider is where your vehicle will be stored. If you have a choice of locations (preferably parked in a friend's or a family member's garage) try to choose a location with the lowest amount of risk. Not only is the type of location (commercial or residential) a factor, but also the actual city and state. If you are unsure, ask your insurance company what their recommendations are. After all, while they would surely prefer getting a higher rate from you, they would most prefer not taking a hit for the loss of your vehicle. When I moved from Florida to Texas, my insurance rates dropped by half. Yet when deciding where to leave my car for a six month period, I chose my father's house in Florida because that was the most secure option. Also, I knew he would start it for me occasionally and drive it around the block, which is important to prevent higher-cost repairs later on.

Utilities

The cost of utilities such as electricity and water obviously depends on usage. If you are planning on closing down your home for the period you are gone, you can most likely arrange a prepayment with your utility company prior to departure. Most companies are willing to work with you to estimate an adequate prepayment amount. Do this in writing and confirm it by phone. Notifying the utility company is a good idea anyway, so that they can keep an eye out for abnormalities and potential safety issues. Your land line can also be prepaid, but once again, make sure you clear this with your phone company.

Obviously, if you will have someone staying at your home, you can choose to make him responsible for paying the utilities in your absence. Utilities, as with most bills, may be paid by a third party without a power of attorney. (Nonetheless, depending on just how many issues you need someone to handle in your absence, a power of attorney is not a bad idea.) Just be sure that the person paying your bills writes the account number and your name in the memo field of each payment check.

Cell Phones

When it comes to your cell phone, you can also arrange to pre-pay your usage. As we discussed in Chapter 3, it's highly preferable to leave your cell phone at home in the first place. If you feel compelled to take one along, bring a prepaid phone instead of your regular phone, and choose a small package. This will force you to be a miser with your minutes, which is a great trait when you are unplugged. Also be sure to downgrade your existing phone to the lowest amount of minutes per month, since you won't be using it. This allows you to maintain the same number and fulfill your contract obligations (if any). You can also prepay your main cell phone since you'll know you won't be exceeding the allotted amount of minutes. This will also be true if you leave your main cell at home and don't bring a prepaid along, which is the ideal situation.

If you will be gone for an extended period and your home will be unoccupied, you may also wish to consider shutting off your cable, satellite, and Internet services. When weighing out this option, keep in mind that reconnection fees can be significant. Therefore, whether you choose to prepay a service you will not be using or pay a significant amount to have it reactivated later will depend on how many months you'll be gone.

Housing

If you're one of the lucky few who can unplug with complete freedom (leaving no house or possessions behind), take a moment to give thanks. The rest of you will have some tough issues to consider, as we discussed in the previous chapter. The most important thing to address is how you will handle paying your mortgage or rent.

While it is likely that your mortgage can be set up for automatic payments, the question of rent is a bit more iffy. This will depend primarily on whether you are paying rent to a corporation or to an individual. If to a corporation, then it's likely they can set up automatic payments for you. If you pay an individual, then you have several choices:

- Set up bill pay in your bank account to generate regular third party deposits to the landlord's account (not available at all banks).

- Write out postdated checks to be mailed or handed to your landlord by a trusted third party. Be sure the person you choose can be counted on! You don't want to come home to a yellow eviction poster taped to your door.

- Give your landlord a series of postdated checks for deposit on certain dates. Make sure you also have your landlord sign an agreement acknowledging receipt of a certain number of checks for a certain amount, each of which may only be deposited on the date on the check.

Car Payment

If you are still making payments on your car, it is best to have these automatically deducted. If you are paying by coupon, either arrange to switch to automatic payments or ask a trusted third party to mail them out. If you go this route, prepare the monthly checks in advance and have the envelopes addressed, stamped, and ready to go. Call your finance company and inquire what information they require with each payment.

Credit Cards

Credit cards are also best handled by automatic payment. Hopefully you've done your best paying off your obligations as directed in Chapter 6, and your credit card bills are minimal. Even if they're all completely paid off before you go, it is highly likely you'll be using a credit card during your travels. Once you've chosen a location and have a good idea of where you'll be going and for how long, try to come up with a monthly estimate of how much you're likely to charge to your credit card. Then plan for that amount to be automatically deducted from your checking account each month. This way, you won't be facing an uncomfortable amount of debt upon your return.

It's a very good idea to notify your credit card company ahead of time that you will be traveling, particularly if you'll be overseas. It's not unheard of for travelers to be stuck someplace because their credit card company didn't know they were abroad and therefore refused to authorize charges. This happened to me while in Africa. I went to check out of a hotel only to find my credit card had been refused. Aside from being embarrassed, I found myself wondering how in the world I was going to pay for something I didn't have enough cash for. Fleeting thoughts of African prisons inspired me to quickly call my credit card company and set the matter straight. Fortunately for me, I was in an area with good infrastructure and I was able to reach them by phone.

Subscriptions

Once again, what to do with subscriptions depends entirely on how long you will be gone. Subscription services such as Netflix should be reduced to the lowest cost plan if you choose to keep them active at all. These types of services typically do not allow you to place them on hold, so you may consider temporarily rerouting them to someone who would enjoy them. Personally, I didn't want to lose the information in my queue and my friends list, so I changed my mailing address to my dad's house. I came back from my sabbatical to find him addicted to Netflix, and now he has his own subscription.

Magazines and newspapers will require a significant amount of lead time to cancel or be rerouted. Three months is the minimum in most cases. It's a good idea to take stock of your current subscriptions and make sure you are not scheduled for automatic renewals.

Storage

If you've decided to pull up stakes and downsize most of your possessions, you're still likely to have some valued possessions to store. If you're unable to store them with a family member (preferred) or trusted friend, then you may have to consider placing your things into storage. The good news is that storage facilities typically offer significant discounts for those paying ahead. Just make sure that if your trip is extended, you don't forget to send additional payments.

Another important consideration is that your possessions have adequate insurance coverage. Since you will have divested yourself of all but the things that matter most to you, don't skimp on the amount of coverage you order. While many of these possessions may have strong sentimental value and are probably irreplaceable, having a little money to spend on some new memories will help soften the blow if you end up with nothing.

Everyone's Favorite Bill

You guessed it—it's your IRS tax bill. You may depart on your journey with no mortgage, no car, and no credit card balances, but there will still be one more bill to pay—your tax bill. Make sure you take this into account when planning your trip. Where will you be on April 15th? If your answer is "unplugged," then make sure that you have filed an extension, or that your accountant is going to file one for you. Naturally, how you handle your tax situation depends on how long you'll be gone, so check the IRS website for information on extensions (or contact your accountant).

Speaking of taxes, this is another reason to consider joining a volunteer organization for at least part of your time off: you could potentially deduct the experience as a charitable expense. If you intend to do this, make sure the organization you are signing up with has 501(c)(3) status. If you're not sure, call them and ask. You should also ask them if the experience is tax deductible.

Accessing Cash While Away

No matter how ascetic an experience you are planning, the reality is that at some point, you will require some cold, hard cash in your hands. Not making reasonable plans for this eventuality can potentially ruin your entire experience, so pay close attention the tips below.

Credit Cards and ATMs

If you will be traveling within the United States, the best plan is to bring one debit card (to use for almost everything) and one credit card (to use only in case of emergencies). If you will be traveling overseas, you may find yourself relying more on your credit cards, even to extract cash from ATMs. Currently, the MasterCard/Cirrus network is the largest in the world. To find out the locations of ATMs worldwide, call 1-800-424-7787. You can use your MasterCard, Maestro, or Cirrus card in any machine displaying any of the three logos, regardless of which of the three is displayed on your card. Another useful tip is to ensure your PIN is only four digits, since PINs with more than four digits will frequently not work overseas.

Traveler's Checks

Traveler's checks are most suited for overseas trips longer than three months in duration. Today, the widespread use of credit cards and availability of ATM machines renders this option almost extinct. That said, carrying traveler's checks is far more secure than carrying copious amounts of cash (they are also easier to conceal), and they are accepted by large banks, exchange bureaus, major shops, and hotels. Traveler's checks from American Express are also refundable if lost or stolen. You can read more about traveler's checks, and even order them, online (see appendix).

Cash on Hand

Whether your destination is domestic or foreign, you need to arrive with some cash on hand. A good rule of thumb is $100 for US destinations and the equivalent of $200 for foreign destinations. Until you are able to get acclimated to your new surroundings and discover the location of the nearest bank or ATM, you'll need money for transportation, forgotten necessities, and food.

If you're traveling overseas, your best bet is to change dollars into the local currency at the destination airport. You'll get the best rate for your dollar on site. Be sure to change it within the airport at an official exchange bureau. Once you have a preliminary amount of cash, your best bet for refills is ATM machines. ATM machines cut out the middle man and result in better rates than exchanging dollars for foreign currency. If you do decide to make extensive use of foreign ATM machines, choose machines located inside of a bank building rather than in an exposed location. In Asia, Africa, and Central America, cloning devices (readers designed to capture your card's information and also your PIN) are prolific. At one company I worked for, an international travel firm, no fewer than three of my coworkers fell prey to this scam in Mexico, and these are people who definitely should have known better. You can never be too careful!

In Case of Emergency

No matter how carefully you plan your trip, you are bound to encounter some type of glitch. Whether this takes the form of a lost or stolen credit card or some other unforeseeable event, you may end up in need of cash—fast.

The good news is that MasterCard and American Express both offer assistance for travelers in distress. If you are traveling more than 100 miles from home, American Express offers 24/7 emergency assistance. They can direct you to English speaking medical and legal professionals, provide emergency cash access, help with lost luggage and passports, and more. MasterCard has a similar program. It is important to note that not all accounts come with all of these benefits, so contact your card company prior to departure to find out exactly what coverage you are qualified for.

Another alternative is having money wired to you by Western Union or MoneyGram. For international destinations, MoneyGram's rates are cheaper. Traditional bank wire transfers are not as recommended. In our post 9/11 world, these transactions can take a week or more to process, depending on the countries involved.

Naturally, in case of a true emergency you can always get in touch with the nearest American embassy or consulate. Rather than searching for this information once you are there, you should have the contact information printed out and stored in a secure place—not with your money. By the way, this also goes for the copy of your passport: make sure you don't store it with your money, or risk losing both at the same time.) The consulate can help put you in touch with friends or family back home and assist you with obtaining emergency cash. It's a very good idea to check in with your local consulate anyway so that they know where to find you in the event of a national emergency (such as political unrest or a natural disaster). See the appendix for assistance locating the appropriate consulate.

Back at the Ranch

Taking care of finances while you are away is a very important consideration, but it's not the only aspect of the life you're leaving to which you'll need to devote some thought. Those of you returning to a permanent residence will have to take some special precautions, especially if your home will be vacant in your absence. The last thing you want to do is unwittingly advertise this fact to thieves or vandals. Those of you pulling up stakes completely will have different considerations as well.

The Paper Trail

Even if you've suspended or canceled newspaper delivery, ask a neighbor to keep an eye out for sporadic stray newspapers. Many local newspapers (especially in small towns) occasionally distribute free issues in order to garner new subscribers. If you live in a subdivision or apartment complex, also ask your neighbor to be on the lookout for flyers or announcements. Other clues for thieves are phone book deliveries left on doorsteps and advertisements from businesses new to your neighborhood, which are often left hanging on your front door knob.

Batten Down the Hatches

If you are leaving a vacant house in your wake, make sure you've literally unplugged— meaning your major appliances (refrigerator, washer, dryer, etc.). A single power surge during a storm could potentially fry all of your electronics. Turn off the water to your washing machine and ice maker. You may wish to leave your air conditioning and heating systems functioning, but keep in mind that the home will be vacant when determining which temperatures to set. The goal is to avoid unhealthy extremes. If you'll be gone longer than three months, ask a friend to check in as the seasons change to make sure these systems are operating properly. During the same visit, they should also flush all of your toilets and open a few windows to let in some fresh air. (It's also not a bad idea to make sure all toilets have been properly flushed before you shut the door behind you. Neither you nor your appointee will be prepared to face something that's been festering for three months or more.)

Invest in timers for at least two lamps (on opposite sides of your home) and have them come on and shut off at random times. Both elements here are key—only having a single light come on in one part of your house, at the same time every day, is not likely to fool anyone.

Inform local law enforcement that you will be out of town for an extended period and whether or not you'll have anyone checking your place. Let them know exactly who this person will be, as well as whom they should contact in case of an emergency at your residence, such as fire, burglary, or vandalism.

The Check Is in the Mail

If you are maintaining a post office box or other mail service, arrange to have a friend pick up mail occasionally and dispose of obvious junk mail (catalogs, credit card solicitations, etc.). Otherwise be prepared to face an overwhelming mountain of paper upon your return.

This is important for another reason as well. While you've given careful thought to your bills, you may have forgotten about another kind of check—one made out to *you*. This could be anything from a long forgotten rebate check, a class action settlement you didn't even know about, or some other totally unpredictable money that will come your way after you've departed. As unlikely as this seems, it's a great idea to leave a couple of deposit slips with a trusted friend or family member so that these checks will not expire before they can be deposited. Many times, the final paycheck from an employer will be a physical check instead of being issued through direct deposit. This is also true of security deposit refunds from landlords and utilities. The latter tend to take several weeks to be processed, so it's highly likely they will arrive in your absence.

If you don't have a post office box, make sure to put a hold on mail delivered to your primary residence. These are usually valid only for thirty days, so if you will be gone longer, it's best to set up a temporary forwarding address (either to a trusted friend or family member's address, or to a rented mailbox service). You can complete a temporary change of address online, but make sure the billing zip code for your credit card (used only for verification) matches the address to which you'll be forwarding mail.

Doug and Cindy's Story

∞

Imagine spending a year in the cramped quarters of a thirty-six foot catamaran with your spouse and your dog as you travel in international waters. Now imagine that this is really your *fourth* year living on the boat—the first three you were anchored outside of your home town, preparing for your journey. Sound daunting? Well, according to Cindy, it wasn't half as daunting as the prospect of living an average life with no surprises.

"I never wanted to live a normal life," she confesses. "I always had a touch of wanderlust and dreamer in me that I inherited from my dad. As a child I loved to read *National Geographic* and I dreamed of seeing the places I read about in the magazine. I always had a feeling of dread about nine-to-five and being at the same job year after year." This dread was accentuated during one of her high school jobs filing papers at a big company. She went to a lunch break party for a man who was retiring after twenty years. His reward for his years of dedication—she was appalled to discover—was pasta salad and a pen.

"Twenty freaking years of his life and he gets deli and a pen. That completely depressed me, but it also lit a fire in me and I promised myself I would never end up like that." After reading *Maiden Voyage* at age twenty, Cindy knew right then her dream was to sail around the world. When she met Doug, they already had a common passion and a common dream.

The bottom line was that they already had a healthy, stable relationship before they unplugged together. "We met many people who did this trip together and ended up breaking up. I'd say around seven out of ten couples broke up by end of the trip, because they were doing this to fix their relationship. Most of the time, one half of the couple was not really into doing the trip, they were just doing it to please the other person."

Although they were following their hearts, they didn't leave their heads out of the equation. Doug and Cindy realized right from the start that the kind of trip they had in mind would require a lot of planning, effort, and sacrifice. They lived off of one income for a long time, using Cindy's salary to pay off expenses and finance their trip. (In the DC area where the couple still lives, this is not an easy undertaking.)

Prior to departing, the couple asked a friend of Cindy's in Atlanta to handle mail for them. They changed everything to her address and signed her on to some bank accounts and other legal and financial accounts. "She is stable, trustworthy, and an accountant, so she was a good choice. She handled paying the few bills we had, she did our taxes, and let us know when we were running out of money. She forwarded mail, made phone calls or emailed on our behalf, and was a point person for other people who wanted to get in touch with us."

When they left they had no cars, no cell phones, no health insurance, no jobs, no debt. They kept just one credit card and one debit card. "We banked on our good health and the fact that one of my brothers is a doctor and hooked us up with enough medical supplies for a small third world village. None of which we needed and we ended up donating it all to a small village in Cuba on our way back to the States."

Before they moved onto the boat they had a small but nice apartment. The week before they moved out, they hosted an "Everything Must Go!" party. "We told our friends to bring boxes and moving vans and have at it. Everything but the dog and our music collection was up for grabs." At the end of the night they found themselves sitting in an empty apartment with Schooner, a box of CDs, and the keys to their new boat. The very next day, they walked down the street to the marina with a suitcase of clothes and moved aboard.

The couple returned from their joint adventure to better jobs, better salaries, increased flexibility and more fun! They also say their relationship is stronger than ever. They are currently saving for another voyage, this time with their new son Zach. They've upgraded to a larger catamaran (44 feet), but still don't maintain a storage space. "We try to keep a rule that if you want one of something, you need to get rid of an equivalent thing. So if I want a pair of shoes, I make myself wait until I have a pair that needs to go to Goodwill. If I want a sweater, I need to get rid of one. And so on. It keeps our expenses down, it keeps the clutter down, and it makes you think about what you really need. I usually end up getting rid of a bag of stuff rather than just an equivalent item. I love downsizing, it's like losing weight!"

Your Furry (or Feathered) Friends

If you are a pet owner, you'll need to make some very important decisions regarding your charges. If you are traveling domestically, it's possible (in a very limited number of cases) to bring your pet with you. This will depend not only on the size, species and personality of your pet, but also on your chosen destination. Use common sense and consideration—is your pet going to be perceived as a threat to others, even in a pet-friendly environment? How is your pet likely to react to change? While dogs can make excellent traveling companions, cats are usually better off left with a close friend or family member. If you have other pets (such as birds or reptiles) it may be considerably harder for you to find temporary accommodations for them in your absence. Ask your vet for recommendations.

If you do leave your pet in someone else's charge, be sure you bring some of the things they are familiar with to their new location. This could be your pet's bedding or blanket, or a shirt with your scent in it. This will make your pet feel far more comfortable during the initial transition period.

It's strongly recommended not to bring your pets on trips to international destinations. Not only can quarantine restrictions be significant, but also health risks and cultural attitudes regarding pets will be different from those Muffy faces at home. As much as you might miss your pet, know that it will be better off with a friend or family member than it would be venturing into foreign territory. Bring a picture, not the pet.

Schooner's Story

∞

Schooner's life truly began when Doug and Cindy brought the Chow-Shepherd mix home from the pound. I asked the couple what it was like bringing along a fifty-pound dog on their seafaring adventure. "Schooner was a pain in the butt," Doug proclaimed. Although Schooner had adapted to life on board the boat, dogs are wired not to relieve themselves in their nesting area. In the three years the boat was anchored in the marina, it was relatively easy to take him for a walk. But "at sea, sometimes your options are limited. One time, we were in an alligator-infested swamp area, and he just would not go on the boat. You see, once we left the dock, the entire boat became his home territory, which he refused to violate. He jumped off the side of the boat and sank right up to his chest."

Other times, it was comforting having a dog on board. After all, the catamaran was not only their mode of transportation but also their home—everything they had left in the world was on board. For this reason, dogs are not uncommon on sailboats. According to Cindy, "He never barks, always stays close by without a leash, and is a good sport in all types of new and crazy scenarios. At the same time, he becomes a loyal and intimidating guard dog when we're not home and anyone tries to get near the boat."

Another positive aspect of having a dog on board was that Schooner was a great ice breaker. "We made many friends and glided through some tricky cultural situations thanks to the friendly, drooling fur ball always at our side. We joke that Schooner is probably the only gringo dog to stroll El Malecon in Havana and sleep on the steps of the Museum of the Revolution. He had his own seat on a cultural bus tour in the Exumas and was invited to spend the night at the largest estate in Nassau. He loved nothing more than peeling coconuts with his teeth and running as fast as he could along the edge of a white sand beach. When other boats would hail us on the radio, rather than calling us by our boat name they just called 'Schooner dog, Schooner dog, this is Wayfarer, do you copy?' Our trip was really more like Schooner's Excellent Adventure!" Cindy laughs.

That said, Cindy still questions their judgment in bringing their dog along in the first place. "The paperwork, trying to find a place to walk him all the time, the extra water and food requirements, and the constant fur balls were a pain. Now that I have a human child as opposed to just a furry one, I think back and wonder what I was thinking dragging that dog from island to island!"

Sailing community message boards include lots of tips for sailing with four-legged friends. Some sailors advise having patches of AstroTurf to avoid mishaps

SCHOONER'S STORY, *cont.*

like Schooner's. Others strongly recommend buying booties to ensure a stronger grip on slippery decks. While lifejackets are an obvious requirement, some sailors also like to make sure their dogs are always clipped to the rails to prevent accidental cases of dog overboard!

These days, Schooner is living out his final years on his family's new forty-four-foot catamaran, currently docked in Annapolis. While he enjoyed his year at sea, he agrees with his family that the last trip was good enough to last him a lifetime.

Consider a Home Exchange

If you find that your list of responsibilities to delegate is as long as this chapter (pets, plants, bills, house, cars, etc.) you may wish to consider participating in a home exchange. This option recently gained press in the 2007 movie *The Holiday*, starring Cameron Diaz and Kate Winslet. The plot involves two women (one from London and one from Los Angeles) who find themselves stuck in dead end relationships and unsatisfying lives. They sign up for a home exchange service, trade lives for a while, and eventually find love.

Exchanging homes can be a perfect solution, not just for single travelers, but also for families and couples wishing to unplug without abandoning their responsibilities. In addition to reducing the costs of unplugging (such as housing and local transportation if a car is part of the exchange), it can also reduce the amount of responsibilities that must be delegated in your absence. Friends or family members are more likely to be willing to look after your possessions and responsibilities if the list is relatively short.

Obviously this option is best suited to those who own their home and plan to return to their point of origin after unplugging.

The appendix section of this book lists the two most well-known home exchange services, which can assist you with domestic as well as international exchanges. If there will be strangers staying in your home, you should take the proper precautions. Both of the websites listed have an FAQ section to guide you, as well as testimonials from dozens of successful exchangers.

One important caveat: just because it's possible to exchange successfully with people who live in big cities that you could otherwise not afford to visit (such as London, Tokyo, or Paris), don't lose sight of the goal of unplugging in a more natural than digital environment. The very last thing you want to do is find yourself in another location with cell phones, television, and the Internet to distract you from your inward journey.

Summary

- Get organized. List your creditors, how frequently they must be paid, and the amounts due.

- Differentiate between bills that should be prepaid and those that can be paid automatically. Contact creditors and utilities to make individual arrangements.

- Contact your credit card companies. Not only should they be aware of your whereabouts (especially for overseas travel) but they can apprise you of special services they offer travelers.

- Adjust your auto insurance to reflect diminished usage and change of venue. Make sure your health insurance will cover you abroad. If not, buy travel health insurance.

- If you must bring a cell phone with you, make it the prepaid variety with minimal minutes. Be sure to downgrade your main cell plan to minimal usage and to prepay it for the months you'll be gone.

- Don't forget about taxes. Be sure you've arranged for an extension if you'll be away on April 15th.

- Research ATM locations and consulate information prior to your departure. Have this information with you (but separate from your cash and other valuables) in case of an emergency.

- Be sure that an empty home is not a target for thieves or vandals in your absence. Leave no clues that the occupant is away, no matter how minor.

- Inform local authorities of your absence and provide instructions in case of emergency.

- Provide for the unlikely arrival of money while you are gone. It's actually not as unlikely as you may think.

- In the vast majority of cases, it's better to bring a photo of your pet rather the pet itself. If you do choose to bring Fido or Fluffy along, research message boards thoroughly for tips from other travelers.

- If the list of responsibilities you must delegate in your absence is overwhelming, you might wish to consider a home exchange service.

Small Steps to Freedom: Writing Exercise

On a sheet of paper, write out all of your weekly, monthly, and annual bills and subscriptions.

Now, on another sheet of paper, create three columns: "Automate," "Delegate," and "Eliminate." Try to fit everything from the first page into one of the three columns.

Think of whom you would choose as the person primarily responsible for the delegated items. Do you have someone reliable, responsible, and trustworthy, as Doug and Cindy did? Or should you consider hiring some type of service?

Chapter Eight

I'm There, Now What?

The All Important Road Map

J UST AS YOU WOULD NEVER UNDERTAKE A LONG ROAD
trip without a map, you should never undertake a
spiritual journey without a journal. This is perhaps the
most important piece of advice in this book—it is the
one thing that will help you achieve your goals not only while
you are gone, but long after your return as well.

The kind of journal I am referring to is not a mere listing of your daily activities. Naturally, you will want to record
exciting or interesting events in your journal, but this should
not be its primary purpose on this type of a trip. Rather, you
want to record more of what you *feel* than of what you *do*.
You should record your fears, your hopes, what you miss from
your old life and what you definitely don't miss. You should
also write about the people you'll meet in your travels, individuals who will inspire you and others who will repel you.
You'll be introduced to career ideas that you never imagined

existed—write about them, even if they don't seem relevant. You will discover skills or abilities that you never knew you had. Write them down.

If you have followed my advice and chosen a location that is totally foreign to you, your initial entries will probably be filled with tinges of fear and even regret. If you've chosen the right experience, you *will* feel doubt—"What have I done?" is a perfectly natural reaction. In most cases, these feelings will last only about a week, which is long enough to start to become acclimated to your new surroundings. During my own experience, I remember having that feeling for about the first forty-eight hours. Then the natural wonders of my environment slowly grabbed hold of my consciousness, and I surrendered to the experience. Personally, I couldn't have undertaken such a long sabbatical if I'd chosen a location in a thriving metropolis, no matter how foreign. For me, the beauty of experiencing the African wildlife, the majestic mountains and the never ending skies filled me with a much needed peace. I couldn't and wouldn't have felt the same way in Johannesburg as I did in the bush. Although each individual is different—and there may be some true city loving people among you—I strongly suggest that you begin your journey in a place that is, indeed, more natural than digital. If you decide to go to Japan, for instance, I recommend starting off at a retreat in the Japanese countryside before heading off to bustling Tokyo. The initial setting for this experience is vital—you will need to be in surroundings that will calm your agitated spirit.

One of the things that will be very helpful is if you start your journal *before* you leave. In these entries you should write, with as much detail as possible, the things in your current lifestyle, job, or relationship that are unsettling to you. You should also write what your expected goals are for this journey. An important caveat: these goals are most definitely fluid. In other words, you may end up with a different set of goals for your life at the conclusion of your experience than the ones with which you began. This is actually a positive sign of growth. There are outcomes and possibilities for each one of us in life that we cannot anticipate or appreciate until we have let go of our existing perceptions, as Dom's story shows. To end up with identical goals at the end of a long term inward journey is either tremendously serendipitous or a sign that the journey was fruitless.

Dom's Story

∞

Ever since his first trip to South America at the age of eighteen, Dom had wanted to visit Central America. He found the culture a refreshing change of pace from his own life in the UK. "The developed world has a lot to learn from the developing world with regard to social issues. The First World has moved on too fast, leaving in its wake its culture and history and the value of family in a deranged search for money," Dom says. In contrast, "family values, as well as a sense of reality, are alive and kicking in the so-called Third World."

Despite his love of Latin American culture, it wasn't until he was faced with a life threatening brain condition in his twenties that Dom decided to leave his job as an emerging markets analyst in London and follow his heart.

After undergoing life saving surgery, he sold his possessions, quit his job, and set out for adventure with his best friend Mike. Their plan simply was to travel and enjoy themselves, eventually opening their own bar somewhere warm.

The duo's plan hit a snag as soon as they arrived in Guatemala. Mike met a beautiful Mexican girl named Lily, and they got married. Dom suddenly found himself operating solo. He traveled a bit longer, then ended up back in Guatemala and got a job managing a bar. One day, a captivating girl named Doreen walked in. "She ordered a banana pie," Dom recalls with a smile.

It became obvious that the two had quite a bit in common: both had university degrees and experience in marketing. However, their relationship was delayed by circumstances. "I needed to raise some serious funds, so I went back to my old job in London for a while."

A few months later, Dom returned to Guatemala, cash and plan in hand. He met up with Doreen, and the couple soon put their collective talents to use by starting their own company, D&D Marketing, which offers business plan and marketing assistance to companies in Guatemala.

While Dom enjoyed his new life and partnership with Doreen, something was missing. After a little soul searching, the couple realized that to stay true to their core values, they should turn their focus to working with the indigenous population. As a native Guatemalan, Doreen wanted to give something back to her community, and Dom wanted to do something more meaningful than he'd been doing in London. Simply changing cities wasn't going to accomplish that.

Around this time Richard, an old friend of Dom's from the UK, showed up in Guatemala.

Richard was in the process of setting up his own company, Global Vision International, which focuses on environmental and community volunteer projects worldwide.

Today, Dom and Doreen—in partnership with Richard's company—have established more than ten schools in Guatemala, Honduras, Ecuador, Peru, and Costa Rica. The schools are important because in most of these countries students must pay to attend elementary school. When faced with a choice of paying for their children's education or using their children as laborers on farms or other projects, most of the indigenous families choose the latter. The schools set up by Dom and Doreen are funded entirely by volunteer donations. Not only do the children receive a basic education, but a nourishing meal as well. The projects are extremely well respected by the communities in which they operate. Santiago, an indigenous community leader, states, "Without knowing how to read or write, a child can't have a secure future; knowing how to read and write, the child's chance for a better job is higher, which helps the whole family." By providing access to free education, the projects have liberated many families from a vicious cycle of illiteracy. In addition, their work with GVI means that they are also providing a service to those from other countries who feel the need to unplug. Dom's projects provide a safe and structured forum for individuals wishing to engage in meaningful volunteer work while spending time in inner reflection.

This year, Dom and Doreen will be cementing another partnership as well—they are getting married. In attendance will be Mike and Lily, with Mike as best man. Although Dom and Mike set out without a road map, they did each find their perfect place in the end.

The reason it is important to enumerate these goals and concerns prior to your journey is that reading them will be immensely helpful during that transitional "What have I done?" phase. As you read over all of the things that you do not like about your life back home, you will be far more likely to give your current adventure the best possible chance.

The human mind has a startling ability to deceive us, primarily out of self preservation. If mothers didn't forget the pain and trauma of childbirth, perhaps many wouldn't have a second child. If we didn't conveniently gloss over the bad parts of unhealthy relationships, it is unlikely that so many of us would keep returning to unsuitable partners. We believe the adage, "The evil we know is better than the evil we don't know." In addition, we seek safety in familiarity; it's part of human nature. Unfortunately, this facet of our personalities is not at all conducive to personal growth.

To prevent yourself from falling into the familiarity trap, you must document all of the negative aspects of your life prior to your departure. If you don't, you run the very real risk of allowing your experience to be sabotaged by this self preservation instinct, of leaving before you give the unknown a chance. After all of your effort in getting here, you don't want this to happen. Remember, contempt for the familiar is what has driven you this far. Don't let familiarity's siren song seduce you back into its clutches.

In addition to helping you survive this transitional period, your journal is an invaluable part of your journey. In order to be effective, you must keep in mind that this document is for you and you alone. You needn't worry about grammar, punctuation, prose or style. As I mentioned in a previous chapter, my own journal was more a compilation of lists and stream of consciousness musings, punctuated by the occasional story, than a traditional "Dear Diary" tome. The margins and front and back covers are also filled with titles of books and music CDs that were suggested to me by fellow travelers.

For your journal to be effective, you need to follow three guidelines:

- Know that you are writing for yourself and yourself only. Do what you have to do to keep it secure upon your return, but make a promise to yourself that you will be totally honest with yourself about everything: the good, the bad, and the ugly. This is usually only possible if you know no other eyes will see it.

- Leave the judge and jury in the suitcase, or better yet, don't bring them along at all! Don't judge what you feel. If you find yourself having a moment of weakness, just live it, don't try to hide it or give yourself grief over it. (This actually applies to more than just your journal, as we'll discuss next.)

- Write as much as possible! This should not be difficult once you realize you don't have to follow a format.

The only journaling convention I suggest you do keep is to write a date with each entry. It will be interesting and useful for you to have an idea of your evolution later on.

Leave the Judge and Jury at Home

According to Sigmund Freud, the human psyche is comprised of three parts: the id, the ego, and the superego. The id is the source of our primitive emotions such as lust, hunger, and rage. The superego is the father figure or authority, which contains our internalized norms, morals, and taboos. The ego mediates between our primitive drives, the super-ego's rules, and the reality of the external world. Our sense of self is primarily derived from the ego and these interactions.

While I am not a psychiatrist or a psychoanalyst, I believe that one of the main problems with our current societal structure is that for most of us, the super-ego has become dominant. Almost everything we do, we do with the knowledge that someone is possibly watching. Those who have seen the movies *Ed TV* or *The Truman Show* have seen this truth from a humorous perspective. We act differently when observed because it is also in our nature to seek approval. Those among us who claim, "I don't care what anybody thinks" are usually lying, myself included. The same can be said of the ubiquitous reality shows, which can't possibly be a reflection of reality because the characters, unlike Truman, know they are being observed. Proof of this abounds: cameras at traffic lights don't even have to be functional in order to have their desired effect.

Another factor that has brought forth the dominance of the super-ego is the advent of instant communications through cell phones, beepers, and wi-fi devices such as Blackberries. Being plugged in to these devices 24/7 also contributes to a sense of always being observed. Gone are the days when a husband would go off on a business trip and call his wife once he arrived at his location, perhaps several days in. Now he's on the phone to her on the way to the airport, at the airport, and for the entire length of his trip. If he's not, he's in trouble! Gone are the days when girlfriends could have a girls' night out with no interruption. Today, I challenge you to go into a nightclub, restaurant, or bar and *not* see the majority of the people there using their cell phones or sending text messages. In fact, it might be easier for you to spot the one person who is not engaging in this kind of activity than it would be to count all of those who are. I'm not suggesting that instant communication has increased fidelity, but it has certainly increased accountability. There is no denying that we act differently when we know we are being observed or monitored.

In Chapter 3, I have already suggested that you leave your phone and wireless system at home, or at least choose a location that will severely limit your ability to use them. Among other previously stated reasons, this is so that you can escape the scrutiny of external judges. The harder part is leaving your internal judge, the super-ego, at home, at least to a certain degree. Of course, I'm not suggesting you go on a hedonistic rampage, but merely that you allow yourself to act, feel, and be who you really are, with no fear of repercussion.

This is also the reason that I suggested that you undertake this journey alone, rather than with a friend or significant other. If the purpose of this trip is to truly discover yourself, you must do so unimpeded by judges, either internal or external. As shown in Chapter 5, it is possible for couples (and even families) to undertake this type of journey successfully, but if and only if they are already settled as individuals and are reconnecting to their inner selves rather than discovering them for the first time.

When most of us look in the mirror, we don't really see ourselves. We see what we strive to present to others. Very few among us are able to look in the mirror and see the complete picture, with defects and imperfections, yet still accept and love our faults as part of who we are. That's because very few people truly know themselves. They spend so much time and effort trying to be appealing to others that the true sense of self, or ego, is lost.

The beauty of undertaking a journey to a distant and unfamiliar place, unencumbered by our existing audience, is that we are free to act as we truly wish. Perhaps your friends know you as the clown of the group and don't take you seriously. Or perhaps you are seen as more of a geek who doesn't know how to have fun. The individuals you will meet in your new surroundings can't possibly have any preconceived ideas of who you are, so you are free to try out a different role. Chances are, if you are yearning to be perceived in a totally different light, this may be the real you wanting to emerge. The problem has been that, until now, you were too afraid of judgment or repercussions to allow the real you to be seen.

Nancy's Story

∞

I'd like to share a funny but true example from my own experience. When I lived and worked in DC, I attended the opera, went to fancy restaurants, and dressed in tailored business suits. I did not own a single pair of jeans. As my husband puts it, I was your typical starched and stuffy Washingtonian. Neither he, nor even my best friend, knew about my secret penchant for watching bull riding on a lazy day. After all, I was hardly a redneck.

NANCY'S STORY, *cont.*

In Africa, there were no such norms that I had to adhere to. I remember going into a ranger's pub in the heart of the bush and hearing Alan Jackson sing *Little Bitty*. My heart lit up with amusement at how the locals enjoyed it as much as the next song, which happened to be by Engelbert Humperdinck. Soon after, Matchbox Twenty's *Unwell* had everyone singing along. Not a person in there appeared fazed by the strange mix of genres, and they all seemed to enjoy each one. I discovered how liberating it was to not be constrained by what you are *supposed* to like. That is the one thing I still miss the most about the bush—fads, fashions, and useless societal conventions don't travel that far.

The person I was in DC was an artificial archetype created to best blend in with my surroundings. I defined myself as an economist, a world traveler, and a gourmand. I watched bull riding in secret and the rest of my life was conducted mostly for the benefit of the outside observer, whoever that happened to be. During this phase of my life, I found myself to be grossly unsatisfied, but I couldn't put my finger on why. I had a reasonably high paying job, an impressive array of friends, and some beautiful possessions. But I could never be myself, for fear of ridicule and failure. It should've been no surprise then that my body rebelled—I was always getting sick. The cycle was vicious as well—bronchitis, pneumonia and strep—at least once a year.

Since returning from my inner journey four years ago, I have barely been touched by any of these illnesses. This is proof that the most wonderful gift you can ever give yourself (as well as to those who love you) is total acceptance of who you are. To this day, I have completely embraced my inner redneck, among other things. My husband and I live in a log cabin high in the mountains with two cats and a senior Great Dane, who makes a fitting hound dog. I dress up and put on makeup only when going out publicly, as opposed to feeling I have to be perfect even if I'm just spending the day at home. I haven't worn pantyhose in four years. To cap it all off, I listen to—gulp!—country music along with almost every other genre imaginable. Whatever I am in the mood for, I do. I have never felt freer.

I'm certainly not suggesting that the country lifestyle is the solution to everyone's problems. I am saying that finding your true self means leaving the judge and jury at home and feeling free to try things you never would under normal circumstances. Despite the country lifestyle being the one that most suits my true personality, I would never have dreamed of trying it while I was trapped in the DC mindset.

Summary

- Don't go on your journey without your road map. Before you leave, start a journal that chronicles your current sources of dissatisfaction, as well as your goals for the journey. Realize that your goals may change.

- Know that your journal is for your eyes only. Be honest!

- Leave your judge and jury at home. This is your chance to try everything freely, with no judgment, in order to discover your true desires, skills, and passions.

Small Steps to Freedom: Writing Exercise

If you haven't already done so for these writing exercises, invest in a journal. Be sure to keep it private.

Under the heading "My Life Today," create two column headings: "Love It" and "Want to Change." Now have a brainstorming session with yourself, listing all of the things you love about your life today, and those things requiring change. This is the most important list you will create. It will guide you before your journey, during your journey, and— most importantly—after your journey.

Chapter Nine

3,2,1 Contact

Staying in Touch with Your Support Base

Y OUR FIRST TASK IS TO DEFINE YOUR SUPPORT
base and whom it includes. The key word here is
"support." Be sure that you will be communicating
only with those who are generally supportive of you and who
particularly believe in your taking this time to unplug. While
you may think you know the individuals who meet these
criteria, you may be surprised to discover differently once you
make your plans known.

Keep in mind that it takes a lot of courage to unplug,
so some of your friends and family may be quite shocked.
It's natural for them to question your decision at first, but
be wary if they persist in being negative long after you've
addressed their concerns. If they can't support your decision,
they shouldn't be included in your support network; it's as
simple as that. This doesn't mean that they are to be permanently excommunicated, but simply that you should not

include them in the list of people you will be communicating with while you are gone.

Unfortunately, due to the complicated nature of human emotions, we often insist on including people in our inner circle whose input merely causes us to question ourselves. Make a promise to yourself to allow only truly supportive individuals in your inner circle. You may be surprised to discover that this circle is very small. It could include your coach or mentor, your closest friend, and a supportive member of your family. The circle may start small, and then expand once others see your plans progressing in a steady, rational manner.

Know Before You Go

While many of the tips in this chapter apply to keeping in touch with your existing friends once you are on your journey, this section deals with making a few useful contacts prior to your departure. If you are planning your trip six months to a year in advance, you'll want to expand your circle of supporters to include those planning similar experiences.

Volunteer Network

If you are going to be spending some time on a volunteer project, ask the group leaders for a list of those participating who are from your general area, or who may be in your same age range. This will serve two purposes. First, it will allow you to get to know one or more fellow volunteers before arriving at the project, thus ensuring at least one friendly face will be waiting for you upon arrival. Second, you will be communicating with someone just as dedicated as you are to the idea of a personal journey. If the rest of your friends and family are making it clear they think this is a hare-brained scheme, you'll at least have one ally to encourage you.

Keep in mind that people you meet during your volunteer experience are likely to become lifelong friends. You'll be experiencing new, exciting, and completely foreign experiences together, regardless of whether your trip takes place in the United States or overseas. As a result, strong bonds are often formed, even in a short period of time. I have several friends I met during my volunteer experiences. Although we were only together for a couple of weeks at a time and the experiences are now several years in my past, these friendships remain meaningful on many levels.

Networking Groups

If you won't be joining a volunteer project, you can still meet like-minded individuals prior to your journey. Networking sites on the Internet abound: MySpace, Facebook, and Friendster to name but a few. Sites like MySpace also have various internal groups you can join, many of which are dedicated to travel. Even if you never meet these group members in person, you can at least connect with other individuals pursuing similar goals. You can read other people's posts and learn from their experiences, as well as encourage each other as you prepare for your trips.

One useful tip is to post questions about a destination to those who have traveled there previously. Many times someone will respond with useful tips and suggestions that you won't find in your standard travel guides.

In addition to Internet networking sites, you can also join networking organizations that host live meetings. Examples include Meetup.com and *Redbook* magazine's women's network. Instead of meeting random individuals you connect with on the Internet, these groups use the Internet to organize group events in public places. If you're the kind of person that prefers personal interactions, this is definitely the safer option.

On the Road

Once you've arrived at your destination, you'll be sorely tempted to have a full-fledged panic attack. "What have I done?" "Why am I here?" and "What should I do now?" are all common reactions. That is why the last thing you need to do is communicate with someone who was not supportive of your plans in the first place. If you do, you may very well find yourself on a plane back home, tail tucked firmly between your legs.

What you really need is to speak to someone who will calm you down and provide much needed encouragement. If you've been communicating with people joining the same volunteer project, you're already one step ahead of the game. They're likely feeling the same feelings and looking forward to receiving your support as well. If you don't have local support, then your support network back at home is even more important.

Email

The simplest, cheapest, and most efficient way to keep in touch, whether domestically or overseas, is by email. Hopefully, however, you're in a location that does not have easy access to email. Ideally, you've also left your computer at home. This means that you will likely be relying on Internet cafes. Internet cafes are actually far more common overseas than they are within the US. While there are many wireless hotspots available in the US, there aren't as many venues offering public computers, other than libraries. If you are unplugging in a remote region of the US, however, it is far more likely that you will find some sort of public access computer available.

Whether you are using a public computer in the US or abroad, there are several important tips you should keep in mind:

- Keep in mind that keyboards are extremely unsanitary objects. They are also equal opportunity germ breeders. On one of my trips to Costa Rica, the entire town came down with a mutant form of conjunctivitis (pink eye). We couldn't figure out how it was spreading so quickly despite our best efforts at sanitation. We soon realized where we'd been falling short—virtually everyone in the town was using the same Internet cafes. Invest in an abundant supply of hand sanitizer, and use it immediately after touching any public surface, especially phones and keyboards.

- Also realize that Internet cafes are prime targets for scam artists. Do not engage in online banking or other sensitive activities at an Internet cafe. If you must check on finances, either do so by phone or have a trusted friend check for you and report back to you.

- To keep costs down, sketch out a rough outline of what you are planning to say prior to arriving at the cafe. Then send a group email to your support network. Since time at the cafe is likely to be limited and trips infrequent, warn your family and friends ahead of time that while you are gone, you will not be sending any messages other than group emails. That way, if you do have time to respond to one or two friends, they will be happy that you made an exception rather than complaining that you didn't write to them enough.

- Prior to departing, create a group address in your web mail address book that includes all of the members of your support network. This way, you won't waste time (and money) entering this information at the cafe. Send an initial message to the group informing them of the exact dates of your journey, emergency access phone numbers, your mailing address, and the fact that you will only be checking email sporadically.

- Set up an auto responder informing everyone else that you are not checking email while you are gone. This way, you are under no obligation to communicate with people who are not part of your support network. Should you receive a message from someone not in your support network, ignore it. Nine times out of ten, you'll be glad you did. Above all, do not engage in communications that could be painful or detrimental to your peace of mind.

Phone Calls

If you are traveling domestically, your best bet for those occasional phone conversations is a prepaid phone card. Phone calls should be used primarily for checking in with concerned family members and the person primarily responsible for keeping your affairs in order. In both cases, you should pre-arrange a time and date for your first call, and then schedule your phone conversations on a case-by-case basis after that. I can tell you from experience that there is nothing more frustrating than finally gaining access to a phone in a remote location, only to have the party on the other end not answer. When you do finally connect, the conversation will likely not be as productive as it could have been. Also, there will be times when you really need to hear a friendly voice, and a matter as simple as not being able to connect will carry far more weight emotionally than it should.

If you are traveling abroad, there are several affordable options for calling home:

- Investigate callback services. These are numbers you can call from any phone. You call the number provided, let it ring once and hang up. The service will immediately call you back with a US dial tone, and prompt you to enter the number you want to call. The rates for callback services are among the cheapest international long distance rates in the world. (See the appendix for more information.)

- Most major phone companies also offer international calling cards. The benefit of using international calling cards is that you will never need to use coins or purchase foreign calling cards in public pay phones, but can simply dial US numbers directly. You can either use a phone card that is tied to your home number (this doesn't work as well when you are planning to pre-pay your utilities) or what is known as a direct billed card. The latter is simply charged directly to a credit card. A word of warning about using international calling cards: use them exclusively for calling between your foreign location and the US. When making local phone calls or calls within the same geographic area (say Costa Rica to Guatemala) it's best to purchase local calling cards on site. Otherwise, you could end up experiencing a minor heart attack when you finally see your credit card bill.

- Consider foreign SIM chips. If you do bring your cell phone along on an international trip, consider purchasing a prepaid local chip instead of racking up an astronomical phone bill. Most countries, especially developing countries, have embraced cell phone technology. You might be surprised at the number of phone centers available to provide this service.

Snail Mail

As much as our society has moved away from sending traditional letters, nothing beats receiving one when you are in the middle of nowhere. If you are going to be gone for an extended period of time (three months to a year) encourage your friends and support network to send you some good old fashioned mail. At volunteer camps, mail call is a truly exciting time.

- Letter writing can be an extremely therapeutic endeavor. In those moments when you find yourself wishing your best friend were right there with you, write a letter! Not only will you feel as if you have shared the experience with someone who matters, but your friend will be surprised and delighted to receive it, I guarantee it.

- For those friends and family members for whom writing a letter is akin to a root canal, suggest that they simply drop you a postcard now and then. Ask them to keep you informed of major events in their lives, or simply share funny stories. Then be sure to reciprocate. Postcards are a great way to make individual people feel remembered and special to you, which might be an issue if you are relying solely on group emails for communication. They are more likely to not mind group emails if you also send them an occasional postcard. Be sure you personalize the postcard to the recipient, don't just write clichés.

- There will likely come a time when you would truly welcome a care package from your family and friends. Maybe you miss Mom's peanut butter cookies, or perhaps you forgot one of your photo filters at home. Keep in mind that care packages sent overseas should be clearly labeled "gifts" in order to avoid import duties. Also be sure to know the restrictions on food and perishable items. For domestic mail, there are fewer restrictions, but be sure to know what they are (i.e. no liquids or hazardous materials). Also keep in mind that when dealing with international mail, the term "snail mail" reaches new heights. Forewarn your friends and family that packages and letters could take weeks to reach you (so they should start sending them right away!).

A Picture Is Worth a Thousand Words

Since communication of any type should be limited during your journey, it's a good idea to pack a small photo album. The album should contain one or two favorite photos of each of the significant people in your life. Whom you choose is entirely up to you, but try to make it as broad a selection as possible. Include friends, loved ones, family, pets, anyone or anything that will put a smile on your face when you most need it. Many times, it's not necessary to hear a loved one's voice after spending some time reflecting on happy memories together.

If a photo ends up sparking painful memories instead of happy ones, deal with this in your journal. Try to focus on the reasons behind the circumstances. Why did you feel hurt or resentful of the situation? Was it truly because of the other person, or was it actually an area of growth for you? You may be surprised at the answer.

As an exercise for your journey, write a letter to each of the people in your album. If they made you happy, tell them why. If you are attempting to resolve a painful situation, tell them why it was painful for you *and then forgive them*. These letters need never to be sent—the effect on you will still be the same.

Anyone who has seen the movie *Eternal Sunshine of the Spotless Mind* has probably wished that they could simply have their own painful memories erased. (In fact, scientists are working on just such a drug now, as reported on the public radio program Radio Lab.) Whether or not you believe man has evolved from apes, there is no question that we are evolving as a species. Natural selection hasn't eliminated painful memories, because they serve a purpose. While it's easy for most of us to agree with this notion in principle, the application is infinitely more challenging. Think about such a memory in your own life. How much energy do you devote to assigning blame to the other party versus seeking the lesson for growth? Your journey can be an excellent time to discover these lessons. Even if you won't be able to banish these memories entirely, their blades will not cut as deeply.

Somewhere in your photo album, include a picture of yourself as a child. This was the version of you without artificial archetypes, who saw no shame in wearing plaid with stripes, and who knew of no limitations to what you could be when you grew up. Celebrate that child! Acknowledge that your future is just as bright and limitless as it was when that photo was taken. The only difference between you and the little girl who wanted to be a ballerina or the boy who wanted to be an astronaut is that. As an adult, you succumbed to other people's prescriptions for what was possible for your life.

Summary

- Clearly define your support network. Include only those who are truly supportive of you, your goals, and your desire to unplug.

- Resist the temptation to communicate with those who have the ability to bring you down emotionally. While you may think that you'll win them over to your way of thinking, it's far more likely they'll cause you to question yourself instead.

- If joining a volunteer project, get in touch with those already at the site, or others joining the project at the same time as you.

- If you are not volunteering, join a networking group, either in an online community or one that conducts live meetings.

- Once you've arrived, limit communications as much as possible with the world you left behind, and focus instead on listening to your heart.

- Don't use Internet cafes for sensitive communications or financial transactions.

- If traveling overseas for an extended period, look into callback services.

- Prior to departing, create a group email address for your support network in a web mail account. Set expectations regarding with whom and how often you will communicate.

- Create an auto-response message to handle email from everyone outside of your support network.

- Pack a photo album containing pictures of the most significant people in your life, and use it when you need to connect to your loved ones. You can also use it as a catalyst for introspection and healing exercises.

- Include a photo of yourself as a child. Celebrate the unlimited possibilities that existed in your heart and mind at that age.

Small Steps to Freedom: Writing Exercise

Locate a photograph of yourself as a child. What were you doing in the photo? Do you remember what you loved back then, what made you giggle? What did you want to be when you grew up?

Now write the child in that photo a letter. If you knew that this child's future depended on the advice you'd give them in this letter, what would you say?

Consider assembling the small photo album that you would take with you on your journey. You might also consider writing each of the people in the album a letter as well, though they need never to be sent.

Chapter Ten

Reconnecting to the Matrix
Coming Back Home

PERHAPS THE MOST DIFFICULT PART OF YOUR JOURNEY
will be your return home. Most people experience a
combination of excitement and dread, eerily similar
to how they felt about undertaking the trip in the first place.
Depending on how long you've been gone and just how
disconnected you've become, the anticipation of creature
comforts like hot showers on demand, air conditioning, and
eating your favorite foods, and seeing your loved ones again
can be very exciting. At the same time, you're likely to feel
some level of dread that upon returning, you will be sucked
back into the life you so wanted to escape.

Your Job
As we discussed in Chapter 8, there is something you can do
to prevent yourself from losing the ground you gained during
your journey. I'm referring, of course, to your road map, or

journal. Just as it will serve to encourage you during the transitional phase of the journey—when you are likely to be experiencing fear and doubt—your journal will also help ease you back into reality without forgetting the truths you have discovered. Before you are lured back to your old job, you may wish to re-read your journal entries about it. Are the things that bothered you still present? It's entirely possible that some (or even all) of the things you did not like about your old job will remain unchanged, but since *you've* evolved, they will no longer bother you.

Nancy's Re-entry Story

∞

Reconnecting proved very hard for me. The problem was that as a self proclaimed realist, I knew I only had so long to achieve a complete lifestyle change before the need for money would draw me back into the corporate environment I had come to loathe. With an advanced degree in economics and over a decade of corporate experience, I knew it would be difficult to find just the right type of job while resisting the lure of a higher salary doing something I hated.

This is where my road map saved me. There were many times that I considered going back to the corporate world, but was stopped cold by rereading my journal entries. In so doing, I came to realize how much I valued three things: being outdoors, living on a flexible schedule, and having time to write. I knew that even though I could make a lot of money back in the corporate world, experience had proven that such an environment would automatically negate all three of those criteria. I also knew that even though I had volunteered on a wildlife project for the last three months, that in itself hardly qualified me as an expert.

During my volunteer experience, I had come up with the idea of starting a US branch of the volunteer company that I was there to support. My background and skills were certainly a good fit for such a scheme, but companies don't make those types of expansion decisions overnight, so I needed something to keep me busy until I could make that happen. I rented a tiny studio apartment on the beach, and took on three part time jobs, one teaching economics at a local community college, one teaching Italian and one working as a "flight attendant" at a butterfly sanctuary. My friends and family weren't surprised by the teaching jobs since they knew how much I love to teach, but they couldn't believe that I would be willing to spend long hours in the Florida sun doing what was essentially security detail, for a quarter of the pay I'd been accustomed to.

It didn't matter. I loved it! Between the three jobs, I had enough flexibility in my schedule to write, as well as enough income to get by as I bided my time waiting for my dream job. Living in the African bush for three months with no electricity has a way of reprioritizing your needs versus your wants. In my tiny apartment, I had just enough creature comforts to make do while I pursued my goal. Ultimately, my perseverance paid off, and I successfully launched the U.S. office almost a year after my return. In that capacity, I have helped

NANCY'S RE-ENTRY STORY, *cont.*

so many others to fulfill their goals through my company's volunteer experiences that their cumulative
satisfaction is worth more to me than the lucrative
positions I turned down along the way.

Your Coworkers

You might be lucky enough not to have to make the type of
sacrifices I did. Perhaps you went on a corporate sabbatical,
or left the door open to a job that you actually look forward
to coming home to. The question for you is not if you will go
back, but how you will reintegrate.

The first thing you must understand is that you have
done something most people wish they had the time, money,
and—most importantly—the courage, to do. There will be
people who will tell you outright that they are jealous, others
who will gripe that they were not selected for the sabbatical,
and others who will mock your time off or complain about the
work they had to do to cover for you. You may be tempted to
dazzle these people with your adventure stories. "And then,
the elephant came charging through the bush!" Don't. Save
your adventures for those in your support network (discussed
in Chapter 9) who really care and are really supportive. The
last thing you want to be known as in your professional circle
is the "spoiled brat who ran off to Africa."

I'm not suggesting that you stay mute about your experience. Rather, be discreet. Maintain a professional attitude,
and focus on how recharged and ready you are to tackle new
responsibilities. Then live up to it. You will earn the respect

of your superiors, and your coworkers will soon forget how threatened they felt.

Your Romantic Relationships

The year in between my return and achieving my ultimate career goal was hardly an easy one. Rather, I faced more challenges to my newfound beliefs than ever before. Not only was I battling the demons of higher pay versus greater satisfaction—my ex-boyfriend chose this time to reappear in my life. Thanks to my journal, I knew exactly what I would be willing to accept in a relationship and what would ultimately make me unhappy, despite my feelings for him. I would read and reread my journal entries, processing the pain I felt from our previous problems, and I reread all the entries that clearly showed me how much I missed him. This allowed me to take things extremely slowly with him while still being willing to give it a try. We began dating and six months later we were engaged. We've now been married over three years, and there are no ghosts of Christmas past haunting our relationship. While I'm pretty sure it still upsets him that I took this journey alone, I know in my heart that our relationship could never have worked if I hadn't.

Many people who hear our story are often (wrongly) inspired not to give up on their own troubled relationships. Frequently, they want to skip to the happy ending we have achieved without truly doing what was necessary to get there. Time and space will not heal all relationships. However, they can result in the truest assessment possible. I liken this to living inside of a wound—it can never heal properly while you are inside it. You have to step outside of it for healing to begin.

The Italian composer most well known for *Volare*, Domenico Modugno sings a song called *La Lontananza*, or

Distance, which roughly translated says:

> Distance is like the wind
> It extinguishes small fires
> But ignites the big ones.

Only time and distance will tell you what kind of fire you have burning, and if it is worthwhile to reignite it, or extinguish it and move on.

Matt's Story

∞

Remember the guy who met someone just before unplugging and was constantly sending her text messages? When he first came back from his journey, he said he still had many unanswered questions, which I didn't find surprising due to his not having fully unplugged. Here's the rest of the story, which does include a happy ending.

Matt is a young information technology professional in the Washington DC area. In his own words, he'd never quite fit the mold of the majority of people in that area. "I never had the normal educational and career oriented goals. In my adult life, people always asked where you went to school or what you do for a living. When they'd ask about college I used to feel slightly ashamed that I had never finished college, even though it was not for me. To me, life is about the experiences you have, such as going on extended trips and meeting new people."

Matt just returned from such an experience, driving 14,000 miles cross country on his Triumph motorcycle. He traveled from Virginia to Alaska, zig-zagging across the map to include stops in Florida and Canada along the way.

For the most part, he enjoyed his adventure, staying here and there with friends in different states. When he reached British Columbia and the official start of the Alaska Highway, the trip turned brutal. "It was cold, rainy, and windy. There were gravel and muddy roads, and a two mile long bridge that was nothing but steel grating. At that point I thought I was insane for attempting this trek." But he kept on, across the rest of the highway, through Fairbanks and then down to Haines. He caught a ferry to Bellingham, Washington, and then began a beeline east, riding across the northern states to get home. After all, he had someone waiting for him.

It's been a year since his trip, so I recently asked Matt if he and the girl on the other end of the cell phone were still together. And what about all those text messages? Matt replied, "She was 'home' for me the entire ten weeks I was on the road. We're thankful that we got to know each other the way we did, without the normal pressures of what to do or how to act in the beginning of a relationship, because we were separated by so much distance. All we had were our voices on the other end of the phone." Most recently, Kim even bought her own motorcycle and they have been going on rides together.

What about Matt's unanswered questions regarding his career choices? First of all, he was lucky that

MATT'S STORY, *cont.*

his employer valued him and missed him during his absence. As a result, he was promoted to the position of director upon his return. Despite this, he still felt vaguely dissatisfied. It took him a while to figure it out, but what he ultimately discovered was that for him, the key to happiness does not lie in his career. As long as he continues to enjoy life and share his experiences with a like-minded partner, that's good enough for him.

Your Friendships

One of the problems you might find yourself facing upon reconnecting to your old life is that there is now a wedge between you and your old friends. In fact, you're probably going to expend more time and energy staying connected with the like-minded people you met on your journey than you will reconnecting with your long time buddies. This is mostly due to the fact that you're likely to be emotionally fired up from your adventures, and will find it difficult to relate to those living in the same old frame of mind. While this is probably only a temporary phenomenon, this is a good time to reassess whether your values and your friends' values are still in sync.

Doug and Cindy experienced this very issue upon their return (see Chapter 7). "It was extremely tough moving from the open ocean back to the beltway system," Doug shared. "That actually felt like the real world out there, and this feels more like an artificial construct." One of the toughest parts of reintegrating was talking to people with a closed mindset.

"Boat people are different," says Cindy. "They're more casual. Everyone is on a first name basis. You could really get to know a guy named Jack, and then later find out from someone else that he is the CEO of a multi-million-dollar company. At sea, everyone is equal."

Initially, the couple chose to only keep the friends that had the same ideals, the same mindset. Having a child has reintroduced them to "the real world," Cindy confided. Parents don't want their kids to be friends with Doug and Cindy's children because they know that the family will be leaving again in a few years.

Your Location

There are two possible outcomes at the conclusion of your journey: you can go back to the life you had, and pursue it with renewed vigor, or you can decide to change everything, starting with where you live. This is perhaps one of the few times in your life you get to choose where you are going to live, because (hopefully) you are coming back completely unhindered by a job, relationship (if you're single), or other baggage.

These days, very few people remain where they were born for the rest of their lives. We are part of a highly mobile society, and the possibilities are limitless when it comes to choosing where to live. If you are the type of person who is likely to undertake the type of journey described in this book, then you are also probably the type of person who is willing to consider moving to a completely new location.

Once again, your road map should provide you with important answers. Your road map should include a list of the pros and cons of your last location and the location where you unplugged. For instance, if you used to live by the beach and loved its tranquility but hated traffic, write "tranquility" under the pros heading and "traffic" under the cons.

Let's say that you unplugged in a mountain setting, and also enjoyed the tranquility but disliked the cold. You would put a star next to "tranquility" and add "cold" to the con side. Brainstorming in this way will allow you to discover that you don't need a beach to experience tranquility, but that you also don't want a setting that has either excessive traffic or cold weather.

Keep in mind that this process is not an instantaneous one—.it will grow and evolve while you are on your journey. In fact, your list is likely to change numerous times as you experience different facets of your new surroundings. What may seem like a refreshing change at first may soon grow tiresome when experienced day after day. (This is yet another reason why a successful journey should last a minimum of a month.)

Once you have returned home, the very first thing you should do is reread this list. How do you feel about it now that you are back in more familiar surroundings? Does it still ring true?

Chances are, it will. Chances are also good that if you don't pull this list out of your road map, you will forget all about it, and then wonder, months or years down the road, why you still feel dissatisfied.

The best thing to do with your list of pros and cons is to read it, digest it, and then copy it onto a single sheet of paper. As you begin your search for a new dwelling, job, and perhaps even state or country, keep the list visible at all times. Remember, these things were important enough to you that you took the time to record them while you were unencumbered by outside pressures. Don't allow the truths you discovered on your journey to be forgotten—keep them in plain sight.

Your Free Time

Your journey is likely to have resulted in many new experiences. By traveling to new places and meeting new people, you might have discovered new hobbies, music, books, philosophies, and tastes. You have also probably rediscovered things you used to love but had forgotten. Make a promise to yourself that you will not forget the things that bring you pleasure. Life is but a series of moments—the key to life is to fill it with moments that bring you joy.

We have a tendency to become victims of our own success, as we spend more and more time at work and less time on leisure and personal goals. It's not uncommon to become so busy with the details of our existence that we forget all about what it is we are actually striving for. The best way to combat this is to maintain an active support network. This can include the very same people who supported you while you were on your journey, but it doesn't have to.

For example, let's say that while you were on your journey you were working with wildlife. While you may not choose to invest time and money in a career change to become a wildlife biologist, you may derive an immense amount of satisfaction volunteering at your local zoo or wildlife park. (Note the use of "volunteering," not "attending." While it seems paradoxical to suggest adding a commitment to volunteer to your new, soon-to-be-busy life, this is really a commitment to doing something for yourself.)

Perhaps part of your journey included working with impoverished children in a third world country. While you definitely can't see yourself becoming a full time teacher upon repatriation, you did enjoy the bonds and relationships you formed with the children you met. In this case, you might consider volunteering for an organization such as Big Brothers Big Sisters.

Both of the above examples do not involve career changes; they are ways to include the best parts of your journey in your new life. By making a firm commitment to volunteer in the areas you have discovered an interest in, you are also effectively creating a new kind of support network—one that ensures you will stay committed to the things that bring you joy.

Your Spiritual Connection

Most people who set off in search of themselves return from their journey spiritually recharged. The central tenets of your belief system may or may not have changed on your journey. The beliefs you hold may or may not conform to any existing structures. Only one thing is certain: if you do nothing to maintain your newfound spiritual awareness, it will eventually fade away. No matter how successful your new life, you will eventually find yourself feeling lost. While each person's spiritual road map may be different, we all require one to live full lives. A truly whole person takes care of her body, stimulates her mind, and feeds her spirit. How you do the latter is up to you, but you must do it.

If you ascribe to a belief system that has organized meeting places, make a firm commitment to yourself and the organization to participate. Even if your beliefs do not fit neatly into a particular organized religion, chances are good that there is a group of people you can discuss your ideas and grow with. Thanks to the Internet, these groups are easy to find (see the appendix).

Your Coach or Mentor

If you were working with a coach or mentor prior to your trip, it's important to keep working with them upon your return. If you are returning to your existing job from a corporate sabbatical, your mentor can help ease you back into your routine, while helping you implement the lessons you've learned from your journey. Schedule some time with your mentor after your return to develop a reintegration strategy together. Not only will this ease your transition and make the changes less intimidating, but also it will help provide a sense of closure to your time off. If you unplugged on your own and were working with a personal coach, you probably have kept in touch along the way and already have an appointment in place for your return. If this is the case, don't let the money and time you've already invested in your coach go to waste. Many times, people make the mistake of thinking that since they've discovered the Key to Life while on their journey, yet another call to their coach is unnecessary. Even if you feel that way, you lose nothing by having one final conversation with your coach. It's likely that your coach will have additional insights for helping you reach the next level of personal growth, as well as tips for implementing your new strategy.

Peter's Story

∞

Peter's epiphany came one night in the summer of 2003. In his early thirties, he was already a highly successful investment banker with a flat in London and an annual income nearing a quarter of a million pounds. He had it all, or so it seemed until he found himself still at the office one summer night at 9 p.m. He had a sudden vision of himself working those kinds of hours for the next twenty years. "No," he thought, "this isn't how I want to spend the rest of my life." Despite that realization, it took him close to two

PETER'S STORY, *cont.*

years to finally pull the plug. "At one point I had six or seven resignation letters in my drawer, all written but never used!"

It took more than the passing of time for Peter to have the courage to take the plunge. First, he read an article in the *Harvard Business Review* that talked about how difficult it is to effect change while staying in one's current environment. The article made him realize that his current job left him with no time or energy to create a new reality. The second catalyst was watching a friend of his finally unplug, for the same reasons. Seeing someone else take the necessary steps to walk away from it all gave Peter the final push he needed.

He sold his flat, resigned from his job, and set off on a trip around the world. He spent time reading inspirational books and writing in his journal, which he used as a tool to help him focus on values. "I was always thinking about how my life would be different when I got back, and visualizing my role models."

Thanks to his job, he had no problems financing his travels. "I earned about £70,000 in deferred bonuses the year I was away, which more than paid for my trip." Instead, Peter's biggest problem was reconnecting to the matrix at journey's end. Especially difficult was realizing that he'd sold the flat he'd called home for so many years. "I had given up my home and had underestimated how important that base was to me. I felt I needed to resolve that before I could get on following my dream."

Peter's transition period was further complicated by a serious back injury he sustained in Australia.

Thus, his first months back in London were spent not only in unfamiliar territory, but also in a dark place emotionally because of his physical disability. "I couldn't take forward my dream for some months and got quite depressed in the end." Adding to Peter's state of mind was the fact that he had met so many other people who had unplugged, but were never able to successfully reintegrate. "I now understand why many people—when they do get out—never manage to get back in. The easiest reaction is to go off for another year!"

As part of his reintegration process, he started working with Clive Prout, The Sabbatical Coach. Working with Clive, he realized the importance of having a vision coupled with a plan. "I have found that having a plan with milestones actually takes pressure off of achieving things, because you know where you are and that it's part of a bigger plan." Peter says that before he developed a detailed plan, "the pressure was just to keep going at 100 miles an hour." Now, he feels much more relaxed about who he is. "I feel like I know myself and what I want out of life, what's important to me." Life itself is a journey, Peter realizes. "There is so much further it can go."

Your Oasis

Whether you are moving to an entirely new location or returning to an old one, it is vitally important that you create an oasis to shelter both the new you and the promises you have made yourself. The next chapter, "Unplugging From the Comfort of Your Own Home," was written both to guide those wishing to unplug without embarking on a physical journey as well as those returning and reconnecting to the matrix.

Permanently Unplugged: Conrad's Story

In Peter's story, he talks about meeting several permanently unplugged people during his travels, those who could never reassimilate once they uprooted, and found themselves continuing to travel forever. This is one of those stories.

Conrad's father was a neurosurgeon. At the age of 54 (the same year Conrad was born) his father broke his wrist and found himself unable to operate. He went back to school and obtained his PhD in Marine Zoology, and began a second career researching South Pacific reef coral. His travels took him to Indonesia, the Philippines, and Guam, among other places. Many times, he took Conrad with him, instilling a wanderlust and love of adventure in his young son.

As a result, Conrad never bought into our current societal system in the first place. His entire adult life has been spent wandering the globe, on what he calls his "walkabout." He's traveled to over a quarter of the countries on the map, never really settling down or plugging in. His two longest commitments were a seven month backpacking trip throughout

India, followed by a three year stay in a housing coop in California while he finished his BS in psychology.

"I work when I need money, I study when I need to learn, I travel when I need to travel." At the age of 38, he has no plans to change. "If I weren't satisfied with this type of life, I wouldn't be doing it," he claims. "That to me is the great mystery of other people: why do they continue to do things that make them unhappy?"

Four years ago, for reasons he still can't explain or understand, Conrad joined the US Army. "I don't know why I joined, I just did. It felt right. It still feels right, but I have learned to accept my own decisions, whether they are right or wrong." Once he was in, he realized immediately that he didn't fit in with his peers. "I was in the Army, but not of the Army." Today, he chalks it up to "another experience, providing me with another facet to my already multifaceted life."

After a three year tour, he resumed living a permanently unplugged lifestyle. Although he says he prefers to live exactly the way he does, he also confided that this lifestyle choice is not easy. "It's like holding a fist for your whole life. You devote energy towards maintaining it. It becomes habit, but it is an unnatural state." Today, he lives in France. Tomorrow, who knows?

Summary

- Have a re-entry plan in place prior to departing. Don't underestimate the value of having a familiar home base to come back to, which means not selling your home if there is any chance you'll be returning to your location. You probably don't want to end up permanently unplugged.

- Read through your journal before returning to your previous situation (employer, relationship, residence). This will prepare you for facing the factors that may have negatively impacted you prior to your journey. It may also prevent you from making the same mistakes twice.

- Tread lightly around your coworkers. More than likely, not everyone will be as thrilled as you are about your experiences. Envy can lead to resentment, which can lead to an unpleasant working environment, no matter how much you love your actual job.

- Don't immediately write off old friendships because they appear boring while you are still on your post-adventure high. Also don't be afraid to reassess whether or not your values and your friends' values are still in sync.

- Keep the spirit of your journey alive. Dedicate some of your valuable free time to pursuing the hobbies and volunteer activities you discovered on your journey. This is especially important for those of you who will not be pursuing a career change, but who instead will be picking up where you left off.

- Feed your soul. Become involved in activities and organizations that are part of your spiritual road map.

Small Steps to Freedom: Writing Exercise

Take a moment to visualize yourself coming back from an amazing but very long journey. What is the most important thing you'd like to find once you came back? Is it more important to find people you care about, or the specific place you call home? Perhaps financial security is the most important factor.

Another way to reach this conclusion is to pretend that a tornado has just picked up your existing home and carried it away. Are you more likely to:

a) be devastated by the loss of your home

b) be okay with it as long as you have the money to compensate for it

c) be okay because you can count on your family and friends?

Your answer to this scenario is important, because it will dictate which kind of re-entry strategy you should have. Draft a version of this strategy, listing the things you feel are absolutely necessary to a stress-free re-entry.

Chapter 11

Unplugging from the Comfort of Your Own Home

S OME OF YOU MAY HAVE ACTUALLY GIVEN THOUGHTFUL consideration to the preceding chapters, while others may have decided to fast forward to the easy part. If you are among the latter group, think again. While it *is* possible to start an unplugging process without embarking on a physical journey, it's actually much more difficult to do. Difficult, but not impossible.

For one thing, you will still be facing the same surroundings, people, relationships, job, coworkers, and thought processes that govern your currently plugged in life. Secondly, it will be much, much more difficult to detach yourself from the technology that currently enslaves you. By this, I mean your television, cell phone, email, and wi-fi devices. Those people who kick off their unplugged journey with a trip to an international or remote location are often forced to give up at least a couple of these items. Those electing to unplug without leaving home or workplace will face far more temptations, both human and technological in nature.

The following guidelines are not only for those wishing to unplug without a sabbatical, but also for those who have returned from a sabbatical and wish to keep sight of the goals and realizations from their journey.

Keep a Journal

Regardless of whether you are embarking upon a physical adventure or an armchair journey, the most important first step is the same: you must keep a journal. In fact, much of the advice in Chapter 8 holds true for you as well. The key things to remember are:

- Protect your privacy. Do what you have to do to ensure that your reflections are for your eyes only. If you feel confident that no one will see what you are writing, it will make it far easier for you to be brutally honest about your feelings. If you can't be brutally honest, a journal—let alone an inward journey—has no purpose.

- Beware of the judge and jury. It's not enough that you protect your thoughts from prying eyes. You must also protect them from the harshest critic of all—yourself. Even if you are currently maintaining a journal, I suggest you put it aside and begin a new one, solely for unplugging. Your first entry should be in the form of a promise that you make to yourself:

  In these pages I will reveal my innermost thoughts, hopes, fears and dreams. I will ban the judge and jury from passing judgment on them. I will write only what is true. This honesty will be my gift to myself—by stripping away the artificial I will discover the person I really am.

Sign it, date it, live it.

- Write as much as possible! As suggested in Chapter 8, the only journaling convention I suggest you adhere to is to write a date with each entry. This way you will have an idea of your progress later on. The first entry you should make after your affirmation is probably the most difficult. In it, you should try to chronicle your current sources of dissatisfaction. You don't have to analyze them, not at first. Just write down what makes you happy and what makes you unhappy. You can even start a two-column page with those entries. Then take a deep breath and just write what flows. You might even be surprised at what comes out.

- Be faithful. Don't give yourself a lot of grief if you miss a day, but try to write *something* in your journal every day. This will be an important part of the process. As you make specific changes in your lifestyle, habits, and perhaps whom you spend your time with, you should document how these changes make you feel.

Catherine's Story

∞

Like many young and highly successful female entrepreneurs, Catherine (not her real name) found herself dealing with a tremendous amount of stress. After having founded two highly successful information technology businesses, her body rebelled. One day, she awakened to find herself completely debilitated, and didn't know why. Her doctors were also mystified; test after test yielded no answers. In fact, the reality was simple—her body was forcing her to unplug.

With no energy to devote to her businesses, she was forced to delegate the vast majority of her tasks to others. Although she had risen to the level of chairman in one company and CEO in the other, she still felt a need to have a hands-on approach with both of them. After all, they were her creations. This was about to change.

Since Catherine's journey inward was forced by circumstances, she did not leave home. She recognized that while her debilitated state held her body captive, her mind could still travel, so she began to explore it.

Due to her background as a business executive, she had grown rather fond of flip charts. She had one brought to her home, and set about creating her own kind of road map. Her success in business gave her the confidence that she could achieve anything she truly wanted. The only question in her mind was "What do I really want?"

She let her mind relax and just decided to write what freely came to mind. "I asked myself: What would make me truly happy?" She realized that while she was successful in many ways, she had still not found love. (Most men found her brains and stunning beauty an intimidating combination.) At the very center of her flip chart, she drew a circle and labeled it "Family." Everything else in her life, she realized, would be secondary. Each week, she delved deeper and deeper into each element of her flow chart, getting more and more specific about how she would accomplish each aspect. By the time her body had mended, she had written down on paper a detailed plan of action for creating the life she truly wanted.

Today, Catherine lives in a medieval European castle with her gorgeous husband (of noble birth) and their newborn son. She is actively involved in her community, but her focus remains on that center circle of her flip chart—her family. You could say it's a fairy tale ending.

Unplug the TV

Okay, perhaps not literally, but it wouldn't be a bad idea. It's truly amazing how much angst is channeled from that little square box. (Or, if you're a true victim of consumerism, that giant, flat box.) Asking some people to stop watching TV is akin to asking them to stop breathing. If you are one of those people, don't despair. I'm not asking you to give up visual entertainment entirely. I'm asking you to give up *television programming.* (This includes syndicated shows, talk shows, news shows, and the most toxic of all: so-called reality shows.)

One of the main goals of unplugging is to free yourself from the consumer driven matrix. How can you possibly do this if you subject yourself to a constant stream of profit-motivated messages?

There are still plenty of things you can watch. Through services such as Netflix, you can rent movies and documentaries cheaply, many of which will be great motivational tools and excellent guides on the path to self discovery. (See the appendix for ideas, or visit the *Unplugged* website—www. unplugyourhead.com—for more.) It *is* possible to use visual media to stimulate your mind rather than clutter it.

Another added benefit is the increased sense of peace you'll achieve by not having the constant noise of television on in the background. Do you know someone who has the TV on day and night, no matter what's on, just for company? Or worse, are you that person? Learning to live in a more tranquil environment will be paramount to a more tranquil you.

If eliminating television from your life entirely seems impossible, try it for just one week. Then document in your journal how this week was spent, what you missed and didn't miss. I'm not advocating that you never watch television again, but to start the unplugging process, this is the first thing you *should* disconnect from.

You will be amazed at how much stress will be eliminated by cutting out the manufactured news and the consumerist propaganda from your life. It's also amazing how much more time you will have that can be devoted to things you really enjoy, instead of spacing out in front of mindless programming.

There are those who might take the view that you are living a sheltered life by not watching the television news. Then there are the more enlightened people, who realize that every message you see on a television screen is paid for by someone, even the news. It's not as if you have isolated yourself completely: you can listen to the hourly news on the radio, routinely check news sites on the Internet, and read the local papers. But you can choose to remove the constant stream of messages and commercials from your living space. This has proven to be extremely liberating. For one thing, you will not be constantly reminded of the next widget or gadget you need to make your life better.

Limit Email and Instant Communications

After eliminating television, this is perhaps the second hardest thing most of us will face. After all, we use email to work, to communicate with friends and family, and for entertainment (you know, those endless jokes and important notices we constantly send and receive).

The beginning of your journey, say the first couple of weeks, is the most important time to follow this bit of advice. In fact, that is true for most of the suggestions in this chapter. None of them are intended to be lifelong restrictions, but rather a series of steps that you should implement during a month-long process. After a month of following these suggestions, you will find yourself in a different place (emotionally) than you currently are, guaranteed. In fact, you may enjoy the feeling so much you may extend it another month, then another, and so on. Once you reach a point where you have more clearly defined your goals, dreams, and desires—yourself, in essence—you may wish to gradually reintroduce some of these elements back into your lifestyle.

The first step to take regarding email is to note just how much time you are actually spending on it. (I use the word "email" here as a catchall term to also include text messages and instant messaging.) After taking note of just how much time you spend in this type of communication, cut it in half. Let's say you check email every half hour, or send a message every half hour. Your goal for your first week is to reduce this to every hour. (The best way to do this is to buy a little timer, instead of a computer based program such as Outlook.) In week two, increase this to every two hours. In week three, increase to every four, etc. Your ultimate goal for your first month is to reach the point where you are checking or responding to email or messages only twice a day.

Obviously, this does not apply to your work email. To keep one from interfering with the other, be sure that you are only using a personal email address for personal communications. By now, you should be aware of the level of spying that most employers engage in on their employees, so you should be doing this anyway. I've known quite a few guys in the IT departments of companies I've worked for, and I can attest that even if your employer doesn't care what you're talking about, *someone* does. Perhaps just the nosy IT guy!

Revamp Your Communication Style

"Wait a minute," you might be saying. "My friends are going to think I'm a complete jerk if I just start ignoring them." Well then, don't! You have two choices—you can either tell your friends about your desire to try to unplug for a while, or you can just start implementing different ways of communicating with them.

With a collection of friends around the world, email truly is the most efficacious method of communicating with them. However, one of the things I brought back from my year long sabbatical in remote parts of the world was a renewed enjoyment of traditional written communications. By this I mean letters and postcards.

- Each week, write one friend a letter. Yes, a real letter. Hand write it. If this is someone you usually email quite a bit, good. If it's someone you've lost touch with, even better. You might find it helpful to keep a pad next to your desk, and when the urge to email this person strikes, jot down a note instead. At the end of your week, you will have enough material for a letter. Not only is letter writing therapeutic, it makes us really think about what we are saying to the other person, and how we are saying it. On the recipient's end, they are likely to be quite pleasantly surprised to receive an old fashioned letter.

- Buy an all-occasion box of cards. Each week, send a card to one of your friends or family (someone other than the person you wrote the letter to, although you may enclose the letter in a card). How many e-cards did you get this past holiday season? Disappointing, wasn't it? There's no denying that a handwritten card implies so much more effort. And the best time to receive one is when you are absolutely not expecting one.

- Have fun with postcards. This is a great method to let someone know we are thinking of him, despite a busy schedule. Sending official greeting cards can start to add up, but postcards are often very reasonable, both to buy and to send. Your local grocery store probably has a stack you walk by every day. There are all kinds of postcards you can buy: humorous, inspirational, scenic, embarrassing—you can even create your own. Since the point is to steer you away from electronic communications for now, though, just make it a point to pick some up on your next shopping trip.

- Schedule a phone conversation. Lately, the only phone conversations people seem to engage in are cell phone conversations, conducted to and from wherever they are scurrying off to next. A good percentage of these conversations seem to consist of "I think I'm going to lose you now," or "Are you still there?" or the infamous "Can you hear me now?" Often we find ourselves having to call a person back at least twice just to finish the last sentence that was cut off by a dropped signal. When was the last time you sat down in a quiet place, and used a land line to make a call? Probably as long ago as you wrote someone a letter, right? Many people don't even have a land line now, so that might be asking too much.

- Your first week, ask one of the people that you normally email or message when would be a good time to call them and get caught up. Then make a point of scheduling this time into your day. Find a quiet place to relax (there won't be any random TV noise if you're following the plan) and focus your attention on the call. Now, you should realize that the other person might not be as considerate as you are. In other words, they may have asked to you call at 8 PM on Wednesday, when in fact they are driving back from a night class on a busy highway. You have two choices here. You can either ask them when they'll actually be home, and if they'll have time to chat with you then, or you can make an effort to engage in meaningful, non-multi-tasking conversation on your end only. This second approach will surely illustrate to you what a waste of time these conversations can be, and might be a good motivator not to be the culprit in the future.

Get Outside!

For those embarking on a physical journey, the most important criterion for selecting a destination is that it be more natural than digital. One of the reasons is that a truly fruitful inner journey requires the least possible distractions. Another, perhaps more significant reason is that inner journeys are not just intellectual exercises, but emotional and spiritual in nature as well.

Regardless of your spiritual beliefs, being part of the great outdoors is the most direct conduit to feeling connected with the universe. George Washington Carver once said, "I love to think of nature as an unlimited broadcasting system, through which God speaks to us every hour, if only we tune in."

Your first goal is to dedicate some time each day to spend outside. Perhaps that hour you spent watching a television show can now be spent:

- Eating al fresco in your own backyard

- Taking a walk around your neighborhood

- Writing in your journal as you sit on your deck

- Stargazing

- Spending your lunch hour at a nearby park

The goal for your daily outing is to keep it simple, so that you won't have any reasons not to do it. Obviously, the weather will influence the activities you choose, but it should never be an excuse to stay inside. Even if you reach the end of your day and you are really, really tired, make the effort to walk outside for a few minutes, gaze at the sky or the furthest point in the distance, and simply clear your mind. No matter how little time you actually spend outside each day, make it count. Pay attention to the small details in your outdoor surroundings that you normally ignore.

In addition to your daily routine, you should also commit half of one day each week to being outside, at least for this first month. If you don't have small kids to consider, the best way to do this is to join a club, or volunteer to help with an outdoor related function in your community. Organizations such as the Sierra Club and Outward Bound have great weekend trips and opportunities to get involved on a community level. Public parks and nature based attractions are always in need of volunteers.

If you have children too young to volunteer, make it a point to take everyone to the local park one weekend day each month. Grab a blanket, a picnic basket, and a Frisbee, and shut off your cell phones. If you are short of ideas on how to spend time outside, call your local Chamber of Commerce and ask them what outdoor activities your town offers. You may find yourself discovering a new hobby that you never would have thought of otherwise, like bird watching, fly fishing or metal detecting.

In most neighborhoods, you can see the same pattern: a garage door opens, a car drives out, and the occupant heads to work. Later that day, the car returns, the garage door opens, and the car disappears. If an alien were to visit our planet, he or she might observe, "You know, these people are all living in boxes. Then they get in their box on wheels, drive to another box (their office), probably spend all day working in front of a box (their computer), then drive home again, disappear back into their box, and sit and watch a box (their televisions) all night." Make a vow to yourself to not be a part of this pattern!

Create a Personal Oasis

This is a very important piece of advice, especially for the city dwellers among you. You may be thinking, "It's fine and good for you to suggest an 'al fresco' dinner on my balcony, if you don't mind the smog and the sirens!" While I still believe you should find a way to get outdoors for a short period every day, and for a longer period every week, for those of you living in noisy environments the quality of your indoor space is equally important.

If you live by yourself, this will be relatively easy. If you share your space with a roommate, significant other, or your family, it could be a little more challenging, especially if you are attempting to unplug by yourself. Hopefully, regardless of your situation, everyone already has well established boundaries.

If you've heeded the advice about unplugging your television, then you are already several degrees closer to being able to create an oasis in your home. Rather than attempting to revamp your entire living space, you should start with one area. Make this a place that is as conducive to relaxation as possible. If you have limited space, you could always choose your bedroom. Others might wish to convert a room into a reading room or a study, or use a sunroom or enclosed balcony. Whichever room you choose, one rule is supreme: always keep it free of clutter. This means bills, to-do lists, laundry, or anything else that will make you feel guilty for not addressing it.

For many people, the bedroom is the least inviting place in their home. It is usually the most cluttered room in the house. It's where they store that unused exercise machine in the corner, perhaps covered with things to be ironed, and where they have books and papers stacked on the floor, and maybe even a television on the dresser. If your bedroom is like this, chances are you probably don't sleep very well at night. After all, the last thing you see at night and the first thing you see in the morning is your life's clutter. So, regardless of whether your bedroom is the room you are choosing to convert, you should definitely de-clutter it. You'll sleep better, and that's important for virtually everything else you do!

Once you have de-cluttered your space, start thinking about color and light. Most of us have a favorite color, even if we feel we are too grown up to admit it. This is a color that makes us happy whenever we look at it. If you own your dwelling, consider painting your room (or one wall of your room) in the hue you associate with happiness. If you are renting, you can always add color with rugs, wall hangings, pillows, etc. Please don't associate this advice with frivolous spending and think of it as part of the consumerist matrix. Consider it an investment instead. Having a space within your home that makes you feel safe and happy can have amazingly restorative powers. Sources for tips on organizing your space and decorating on a frugal budget can be found in the appendix of this book.

The lighting you choose is very important. You want two options here. One soft light option, and one over-the-chair style reading light. There will be times when you will want a soothing low light environment to listen to music or just meditate, and other times you will want to escape to your oasis to read a good motivational or inspirational book. An excellent option for the reading light is a lamp designed to simulate natural sunlight. This is far easier on your eyes.

A word about fluorescent lighting—while definitely more economical and long lasting than traditional bulbs, fluorescent lighting also emits a constant series of flickers. For those people who can actually detect these flickers, they can lead to headaches, dizziness, and just a general feeling of being unsettled. If you can't eliminate fluorescent lighting throughout your home, at least eliminate it from your oasis.

What would an oasis be without water? The gentle sound of a stream or of surf hitting sand can be very calming. A simple way to incorporate some water into your oasis, along with a definite change in atmosphere, is a small water (or mist) fountain. You can find several of these on the market for around $20.

Sound itself is a very important concept for an oasis. You want to be able to accomplish two things: eliminate extraneous noises, but enjoy soothing ones as well. For those living in noisy neighborhoods, you may wish to consider purchasing a set of noise canceling headphones or an unobtrusive white noise machine. A CD player and a decent selection of instrumental music are also good worthwhile suggestions. Visit the *Unplugged* website (www.unplugyourhead.com) for suggested titles.

When you are spending time in your oasis, you want to minimize all distractions. To me, sound can be the most invasive distraction of all, so I do everything in my power to minimize sound intrusions in my home. Do the same, it will really make a difference!

Finally, you want to be sure you have a comfortable place to sit while in your oasis. Even if this is your bedroom, you should invest in a comfortable chair for reading, writing in your journal, or just meditating. Ensure that the items in the line of sight of your chair are things you enjoy looking at: a lush plant, a favorite photo, or the wall you painted in your favorite color. If you have an unobstructed view of the outdoors (or even a lighted cityscape), perhaps you want to face that. Do not have it face the door. You want to focus on your inner journey, not what lies beyond the door to your sanctuary.

To summarize, your oasis should:

- Be free of clutter

- Incorporate a color that pleases you

- Use lighting that is conducive to meditation and relaxation

- Be free of sound intrusions but have soothing sounds available, such as that of a water fountain

- Include a comfortable place to sit, with a carefully orchestrated line of sight

Shake Up Your Social Life

Getting unplugged does not mean becoming disconnected from others. Actually, by freeing up your time, eliminating television, revamping your communication style to include scheduled phone calls and handwritten letters, and volunteering outdoors or joining a nature based club, you are likely to form deeper and more meaningful connections than the ones you established previously.

The goal is to remove the artificial connections and establish some real ones. At the conclusion of your first month of being unplugged, schedule a social get together with a wide circle of friends and acquaintances. It's not important to host the activity at your place, but it is important to schedule it somewhere out of the ordinary. In particular, don't schedule it at a restaurant or bar. There are three main criteria your event should follow:

- It should be interactive instead of passive. Getting a large group together for a bowl-a-thon or miniature golf tournament is a better idea than going with a group to a movie. Host a wine or cheese tasting, or throw a mystery dinner party.

- It should involve teaching or learning a new skill. If you are good at making homemade pasta, offer to throw a pasta making party. Each person can bring her own filling, and you can make ravioli in an assembly line. This concept works well for homemade pizza, sushi, etc. (Just don't poison anyone.)

- It should expand your social circle. Ask each friend you have to invite one of their friends or acquaintances that you don't know. Each new person you meet brings with them the opportunity to learn about new hobbies, music, authors, movies, and philosophies that you may not have known about before.

Our world is growing increasingly antisocial. Pretty soon you will not *have* to leave your house to do anything. Today, you can shop online, meet people online, read books online, work online, find a pet online, watch movies online, listen to music online, take classes online, date online. I'm pretty sure someday soon we'll even be able to get married online (without having really met the other person).

When we do emerge from our boxes, we're guaranteed to have cell phones pressed to our ears (or worse, miniature headsets, which make us *look* approachable when in fact we are immersed in our own little worlds). We drive with our car windows up, blasting our own music, or listening to political propaganda. Outdoors, we are frequently spotted plugged into our music systems, listening to our endless collections of downloaded music or podcasts of shows we missed.

The above does not mean that I am against all such technology. As I mentioned in a previous chapter, technology actually helps me to stay unplugged by allowing me to work from home rather than a cubicle. However, I can't help but notice that it is also making each of us more and more self contained. The advent of the Internet brought forth MySpace, Google, and Wikipedia—so do we really need interaction from other humans? Yes! It is a proven fact that a human baby cannot survive without being touched. In fact, people who go long periods of time without touch are more prone to illness, and will actually have a shortened life span.

Not only do our bodies require touch, our minds require human interaction. You may mistakenly believe that limiting your interactions to a self contained world makes you more of an individual. In fact, the opposite is true. Being fully self contained while being fed by downloadable sources actually makes you more of a droid than an individual. You are operating solely on information that is input to your brain and not on knowledge gained through interaction or debate.

Socrates, the founder of Western ethics and moral philosophy, established a method of inquiry known today as the Socratic Method. This technique requires at least two participants, who challenge each other's answers to a given question in order to arrive at the truth. The goal is to force the other party into making a statement that validates your own point of view rather than your opponent's. This is considered true learning.

When we become too self contained, we lose our desire to question. When we lose the desire to question, we lose our individuality. When we lose our individuality, we lose everything.

Mike's Story

∞

In late 2003, Mike found himself sitting on the beach in Lake Tahoe perusing an issue of *Outside Magazine*. "It was a nice article about people pursuing careers that they were passionate about—that they loved. I remarked about these folks to my wife and that the application of that thought to my own life was no less than absurd at the time." At this point in his life, Mike was stuck in a well paid financial consulting job with a large computer company in Silicon Valley. He was bored by his work and lived in cubicle hell. "Mostly I was burned out on what I had been doing for twenty years and my passion for finance and accounting had dried up to a cinder. People around me could tell that. Bosses could tell that. I was truly going through the motions." Mike shares that, despite being handsomely paid, he was "stultified in a gray cubicle working as a faceless minion in an enormous corporation." As a consultant, he felt his fate was tenuous at best. "Worse for me was not knowing what would happen next—a long series of fruitless job interviews? Another cubicle gig with an awful commute?" Mike determined to take control of the next phase of his life and to be miserable no longer.

The article also mentioned the name of a sabbatical coach, so Mike decided to give him a call. Mike worked with Clive for six months, without ever leaving home. The reasons he chose this path were the same reasons he had given up on his entrepreneurial dreams. "Some of this was driven by the needs of my family and my wife's desire for security and predictability. Some was driven by my own indecision and sloth. Some was driven by the fact that I was plotting my Bay Area exit around the purchase of an accounting firm." When he realized that the latter option was pointless due to his growing apathy for finance and taxes, he reluctantly gave up on that idea.

Inspired by the *Outside Magazine* article and his talks with Clive, Mike decided to pursue his dream: transforming his love of winemaking into his avocation. "I spent lots of time and mental energy on weekly phone calls from Clive on vision and values, on goals, and what was important to me and what was in the way." In early 2006, Mike and his wife bought a franchise business. Within just a few months, their business grew rapidly, and it was earning him more than the full time job he had left. He now had the freedom to control his own schedule, and he had moved out of Silicon Valley. He and his wife found a winery to lease, complete with tasting room, and bought a new house nearby.

Mike's passion for winemaking is evident in the resulting wines. "Our last event was our largest since our inception weekend. We even outsold our host winery at the tasting room in May." The winery was also awarded a couple of silver medals at the El Dorado County Fair in the new wine category.

Thanks to his coaching sessions, he was able to break free of his old job and create a new opportunity. Thanks to the new opportunity, he's been able to "convert the winery from an overblown hobby to a real business." Thanks to all of that, he is now

MIKE'S STORY, *cont.*

the kind of person he read about that summer day in *Outside Magazine*: someone wholeheartedly pursuing what he loves.

Summary

- Keep a journal, and be honest and faithful to it.

- Unplug your television.

- Limit email and instant communications.

- Revamp your communication style to include cards, letters, and scheduled phone conversations.

- Get outside! Incorporate time outdoors on a daily and weekly basis, and pay attention.

- Create a personal oasis.

- Shake up your social life: plan activities that are interactive. Expand your skill set and enlarge your circle of acquaintances (thus your knowledge base).

- Consider hiring a personal coach as discussed in Chapter 4.

Small Steps to Freedom: Writing Exercise

Quick, what is your favorite color? You can't think about it for more than five seconds. No situational answers, either. Just pick a color. Now, list all of the things you can think of that are this color. Next to each one, write a word that describes how that item makes you feel.

Take a look around you, especially if you are in a room that you spend a lot of time in. Is there anything, anything at all, in this room that is this color? If you're like most people, ironically, the answer is no. The color you chose, if you chose quickly, is the color of your childhood. As we grow older, we tend to edit our choices. Our desire to exhibit good taste in our décor and clothing often translates to no longer surrounding ourselves with the things that make us happy.

For your oasis, consider painting an accent wall in a shade of the color you chose. Although that is the option with the most impact, it may not be feasible for you (especially if you are a renter). Instead, take a look at the list you created, and find a way to bring some of those items into your space.

Afterword

Every day you may make progress. Every step may be fruitful. Yet there will stretch out before you an ever lengthening, ever ascending, ever improving path. You know you will never get to the end of the journey. But this, so far from discouraging, only adds to the joy and glory of the climb.

—*Sir Winston Churchill (1874-1965)*

WHETHER YOU CHOOSE TO UNPLUG ON A PHYSICAL journey or from the comfort of home, the end result will be the same. Following the steps outlined in this book will have a transforming effect, not only on your own life, but on the lives of those around you as well.

No matter how you calculate it, life as we know it is precious and short. Ask yourself whether you want to continue living it on someone else's terms—or your own.

No single book, documentary, philosophy, or fad holds all of the answers for everyone. Rather, the answers you seek can only be found through an inward journey. You will face your greatest desires as well as your biggest fears, requiring a kind of courage possessed by few. There will be protracted periods of solitude, although you will never be truly alone. While this is not an endeavor without risk, the rewards are incalculable.

Appendix: Resources

Books

The Alchemist, by Paulo Coelho. (New York: HarperCollins, 2006). This story is really a beautifully told parable that will provide anyone with the inspiration to embark on a personal journey. Through the eyes of Santiago, a Spanish shepherd who leaves his flock to pursue his dreams of treasure in Egypt, we learn what it truly means to embark on not just a journey, but a pilgrimage. Highly recommended reading.

Authentic: How to Make a Living by Being Yourself, by Neil Crofts. (Sussex, United Kingdom: Wiley, 2003). Part memoir, part how-to, this book will inspire you to examine the difference between what you are doing and what you want to do. An excellent book to take along with you on your journey.

The Back Door Guide to Short Term Job Adventures, Internships, Summer Jobs, Seasonal Work, Volunteer Vacations, and Transitions Abroad (Paperback) by Michael Landes. (Berkeley, CA: Ten Speed Press, 2005). This book is an excellent resource for those who truly need a career break, but don't have a clue where to start. With over 1,000 opportunities to try something totally new, you're bound to find some inspiration here.

Do's and Taboos Around the World, edited by Roger E. Axtell (New York: John Wiley and Sons, 1993). This oldie but goodie contains a treasure trove of information designed to prevent you from making embarrassing gaffes while exploring new cultures.

Europe's Monastery and Convent Guesthouses by Kevin J. Wright. (Liguori, MO: Liguori Publications, 2004). A complete guide to monasteries and convent guest houses throughout Europe.

Healing Centers and Retreats by Jennifer Miller. (Santa Fe, NM: John Muir Publications, 1998). Includes a directory for all fifty states and Canada as well as international locations.

International Directory of Voluntary Work by Louise Whetter and Victoria Pybus (Princeton, NJ: Vacation-Work, 2007). A comprehensive guide to a plethora of volunteering opportunities.

Peterson's Learning Adventures Around the World, edited by Peter S. Greenberg (Princeton, NJ: Peterson's, updated yearly). Excellent resource for finding unique travel, volunteer, and work experiences around the globe.

Sanctuaries: The Complete United States. A Guide to Lodging in Abbeys, Monasteries, and Retreats by Jack and Marcia Kelly (New York: Harmony Books, 1996).

So You Want to Join the Peace Corps by Dillon Banerjee. (Berkeley, CA: Ten Speed Press, 2000). For those considering unplugging for longer than one year, this book provides a frank look at the process and benefits of joining the Peace Corps.

Teaching English Abroad, 7th Edition by Susan Griffith. (United Kingdom: Vacation Work, 2005). All the information you need on everything from training to finding a job. Also provides an extensive country-by-country listing of language schools.

Coaching Services

The Sabbatical Coach: www.thesabbaticalcoach.com

Clothing and Equipment for the Traveler

REI: www.rei.com

Sahalie: www.sahalie.com

Travel Smith: www.travelsmith.com

Films

Get inspired to unplug with the following films.

Life or Something Like It (2002, PG-13). This quirky movie stars Angelina Jolie as a materialistic news reporter with aspirations of grandeur. When a psychic predicts her impending death, she undergoes a life transforming change of heart. Ed Burns plays her cameraman and love interest, and teaches her to live a more unplugged lifestyle.

The Matrix (1999, R). This film can be viewed in one of two ways: purely as a science fiction story, or as a parable for our current lives—living within and feeding the consumer driven matrix of our society.

The Motorcycle Diaries (1994, R, English subtitles). This film shows one of history's most famous personages, Che Guevara, as he unplugs and finds his true calling. Regardless of your political affiliations, this is a truly inspiring film that aptly illustrates the joys, hardships, and lessons involved when embarking upon a personal journey.

Now, Voyager. (1943, UR) This Academy Award winning film stars Bette Davis as a woman who leaves it all behind to find love, fulfillment, and meaning on an oceanic voyage. A multilayered gem with multiple messages to inspire you.

General Travel

These insurers offer travel insurance, trip cancellation protection, and coverage for lost baggage and travel accidents. Medical coverage for short term trips is also offered.

Access America, Inc. PO Box 90315 Richmond, VA 23286-4991. (800) 284-8300. Web: www.accessamerica.com

Travel Guard International. 1145 Clark Street, Stevens Point, WI 54481. (800) 782-5151. Web: www.travelguard.com

Traveling with your pet? Check out www.petsonthego.com for information on domestic and international travel requirements as well as a comprehensive directory of pet friendly destinations. (Note: don't think that if you are staying within the United States your pet is allowed to travel freely. Restrictions and regulations also apply to you.)

You can also check out the USDA's website link for pet travel at www.aphis.usda.gov/animal_welfare/pet_travel/pet_travel.shtml

International Travel

Whether you are a US citizen wishing to travel abroad or a foreign citizen wishing to visit the US, the first place to start planning your trip is the State Department's website: www.travel.state.gov. Here you'll find information on passports, visa requirements, and a country-by-country index.

Make sure you apply for a passport at least three months ahead of time in order to avoid hefty expediting fees. If you already have a passport, make sure it will be valid for at least six months after your return to the U.S. (this is a requirement of many countries).

The CIA World Factbook is your best source of information on a country's history, politics, and economy. You can access it free at: https://www.cia.gov/library/publications/the-world-factbook/index.html.

If you will be joining a volunteer project, it is important to enter the country as a *tourist*. For many countries, mentioning that you will be engaging in any type of work, including unpaid volunteer work, will result in lengthy and expensive complications. Sometimes, your entry will even be denied. It's usually far easier to extend your visa once you are in country. Check with your volunteer organization for their suggestions, which will likely vary from country to country.

It advisable to bring good quality photocopies of your passport for identification purposes. This will allow you to leave your passport in a safe place instead of carrying it on your person. You should also leave a copy with a friend or family member back at home.

Upon arriving in a country, check in with the local embassy. For worldwide listings of embassies, visit www. embassyworld.com.

Keep abreast of the latest travel restrictions at the Transportation Security Administration's website: www.tsa.gov.

Download the free booklet, *Know Before You Go*, from the U.S. Customs and Border Protection service at www.cbp. gov. This booklet is an excellent resource for understanding what you can and can't bring back from your travels, and includes several other useful checklists and resources.

Planning on driving overseas? Check out www.thenac. com/international_driving_permit.pdf for information on whether or not you'll need to obtain an international driver's license. This information is also available on www.aaa.com.

The Centers for Disease Control website has an excellent travel resource at www.cdc.gov/travel/default.aspx. Here you can find information on everything from country-specific vaccinations and outbreaks, to general tips for traveling with children and pets. Two highly useful links on this page are the traveler's health kit, and a section devoted to pre- and post-travel general health recommendations.

A word about vaccinations: it's important to begin researching required immunizations at least six months before your intended departure. Many immunizations require booster shots several months after the initial injection, or must be given in a series. Your local county health department is actually your best resource for these types of questions, even if you live in a small town. Ask for the travel desk when you call.

Volunteer Organizations

If you're considering joining a volunteer project, choose your program with care. The following are highly reputable and well-known organizations, but there are literally hundreds of others to consider. When choosing an organization, it's advisable to request contact information for previous volunteers. It's also important to determine whether or not the organization has actual representation and staff on the ground as opposed to being simply being an intermediary.

Doctors without Borders (www.doctorswithoutborders.org). Whether you are a doctor or an administrative professional, you can help save lives overseas. Field work positions are available for both types of volunteers, with preference given to those who can commit to at least six months. (Most administrative positions require a one year commitment.) Conversational ability in French is currently in high demand for former French colonies in Africa.

Habitat for Humanity (www.habitat.org/getinv/volunteer_ programs.aspx). This organization offers a multitude of opportunities, from meaningful vacations to disaster relief. Once you've returned from your trip, you can continue to volunteer in your own back yard as well.

Global Vision International (www.gviusa.com). Whether you'd like to volunteer with indigenous communities or with wildlife, GVI has a program for you. Specializing in longer term programs, (usually at least one month in duration), this private organization is funded entirely by volunteer donations. Although you will pay a significant fee for your participation, the organization offers unique experiences that are not otherwise available to the general public.

Green Volunteers (www.greenvolunteers.org). Website and guide for over 500 different volunteering organizations dedicated to wildlife and conservation projects. Organizations have been vetted by Green Volunteers, and free updates are available by emailing network@greenvolunteers.com. Also has links to Archaeo-Volunteers (archeological and cultural heritage volunteer opportunities) and World Volunteers (humanitarian volunteer projects).

The Peace Corps (www.peacecorps.gov). For those interested in longer term travels: the minimum assignment is 27 months.

Volunteer Abroad Directory (www.volunteerabroad.com. Searchable online directory of hundreds of volunteer opportunities. Most are fee based.

Retreats and Outdoor Adventures

Online directory of nature retreats: www.retreatsonline.com/nature.htm.
Nurture Through Nature: www.ntnretreats.com. Retreats and custom getaways for women.

Outward Bound Wilderness: www.outwardboundwilderness.org. This organization offers wilderness courses from one week on up, with a focus on personal improvement and mastering challenges.

Sierra Club: www.sierraclub.org/outings. Choose from a wide variety of active, outdoor focused getaways.

Other Useful Websites

Teaching overseas: www.teachabroad.com. Includes links to online teacher training, TEFL placement, and a personal assessment test to see if this is a good option for you.

Comprehensive information on traveling and living overseas, including tips from expatriate residents: www.escapeart ist.com

If you're traveling alone, check out www.1yearout.com. This site was created primarily as a resource for those taking a gap year or career break on their own. The site includes a comprehensive listing of hostels, budget accommodation, campsites, sporting activities, tours, and events for planning your adventure. Telephone numbers are included where available, as are websites. 1 Year Out.com believes you should "make sure you experience everything on offer first time round. The world has so much to explore, chances are you might not travel to the same place again, no matter how much you intend to go back."

If you own your home and don't want to abandon it while you are unplugged, you might consider one of the two major home exchange programs. This option is great for those with pets, plants, or other obligations they can't easily delegate.
   HomeLink: www.swapnow.com. Home Link has been offering international home exchanges since 1953. It has been featured in *Time*, the *LA Times*, and *Fodor's* guides. An annual membership is currently $90, but their online directory is free for searching. Maintains offices in over thirty countries.
   International Home Exchange Network: www.home exchange.com. Offers both international and domestic

home exchange programs. Includes over 15,000 worldwide listings.

Unplug Your Head: www.unplugyourhead.com. This is the companion website to the book, featuring tips, a link to the MySpace community, success stories, and a free monthly newsletter.

About the Author

Nancy Whitney Reiter is a former economist and corporate market analyst. As a 9/11 survivor and Generation Xer, she found herself questioning the true meaning of "success," and embarked on a year long travel sabbatical. Her travels took her to Costa Rica and South Africa, where she worked as a volunteer teacher and wildlife researcher. Thanks to this unhampered time of reflection, she decided to abandon the corporate lifestyle in order to pursue her true passions: nature, teaching, and writing.

She is currently a consultant for Global Vision International, an adventure travel company that specializes in long-term travel experiences. Through her work at GVI, she has helped numerous individuals to disconnect and find themselves.

Nancy Whitney Reiter has a BS in economics and international studies from University of South Florida. She also has a MA in economics from University of South Florida. She currently resides in Dewey, Arizona, near Prescott. Her website is www.unplugyourhead.com.

Photo: Greg Reiter

Sentient Publications, LLC publishes books on cultural creativity, experimental education, transformative spirituality, holistic health, new science, ecology, and other topics, approached from an integral viewpoint. Our authors are intensely interested in exploring the nature of life from fresh perspectives, addressing life's great questions, and fostering the full expression of the human potential. Sentient Publications' books arise from the spirit of inquiry and the richness of the inherent dialogue between writer and reader.

Our Culture Tools series is designed to give social catalyzers and cultural entrepreneurs the essential information, technology, and inspiration to forge a sustainable, creative, and compassionate world.

We are very interested in hearing from our readers. To direct suggestions or comments to us, or to be added to our mailing list, please contact:

SENTIENT PUBLICATIONS, LLC
1113 Spruce Street
Boulder, CO 80302
303-443-2188
contact@sentientpublications.com
www.sentientpublications.com